HEARING GOD IN POETRY

Fifty poems for Lent and Easter

Richard Harries

First published in Great Britain in 2021

Society for Promoting Christian Knowledge
36 Causton Street
London SW1P 4ST
www.spck.org.uk

British Library Cataloguing-in-Publication Data
A catalogue record for this book is available from the British Library

ISBN 978–0–281–08629–0
eBook ISBN 978–0–281–08630–6

Typeset by Manila Typesetting Company
First printed in Great Britain by Jellyfish Print Solutions
Subsequently digitally printed in Great Britain

eBook by Manila Typesetting Company

Produced on paper from sustainable forests

For Gyles and Michèle,
who lift the spirits of the nation

Contents

Contents

Contents

Contents

Easter and into the new life in Christ

Acknowledgements

The publisher and author acknowledge with thanks permission to reproduce extracts from the following:

Geoffrey Hill, 'Lachrimae Amantis': from *Tenebrae* by Geoffrey Hill, Andre Deutsch Ltd, London, 1978. Permission sought.

W. H. Auden, 'In Memory of W. B. Yeats' (extract): Copyright © 1939 by W. H. Auden, renewed. Reprinted by permission of Curtis Brown, Ltd. All rights reserved.

Elizabeth Jennings, 'I Count the Moments': from *The Collected Poems* by Elizabeth Jennings (Carcanet Press), reproduced by permission of David Higham Associates.

Les Murray, 'The Quality of Sprawl': from *New Collected Poems* (2003) by Les Murray, reprinted by kind permission of Carcanet Press, Manchester, UK.

R. S. Thomas, 'The Moor': from *Collected Poems: 1945–1990* by R. S. Thomas. Copyright © R. S. Thomas. Reprinted by permission of the Orion Publishing Group, London.

Carol Ann Duffy, 'Prayer': from *Mean Time* by Carol Ann Duffy. Published by Picador. Copyright © Carol Ann Duffy. Reproduced by permission of the author c/o Rogers, Coleridge & White Ltd., 20 Powis Mews, London W11 1JN.

Yehuda Amichai, 'And That Is Your Glory': from *The Selected Poetry of Yehuda Amichai*, by Yehuda Amichai, translated by Chana Bloch and Stephen Mitchell, with a New Foreword by C. K. Williams, © 1986, 1996, 2013 by Chana Bloch and Stephen Mitchell. Published by the University of California Press.

Lucille Clifton, 'oh antic god': from *How to Carry Water: Selected Poems*. Copyright © 2004 2004 by Lucille Clifton. Reprinted with the permission of The Permissions Company, LLC on behalf of BOA Editions, Ltd., boaeditions.org.

Jon Stallworthy, 'The Almond Tree': from *Rounding the Horn: Collected Poems* (1998) by Jon Stallworthy, reprinted by kind permission of Carcanet Press, Manchester, UK.

C. Day-Lewis, 'Walking Away': permission to reproduce sought from Peters Fraser and Dunlop on behalf of the estate of C. Day-Lewis.

Langston Hughes, 'Mother to Son': from *The Collected Poems of Langston Hughes* by Langston Hughes (Alfred A Knopf Inc/ Vintage), reproduced by permission of David Higham Associates.

Seamus Heaney, 'Digging': from *Death of a Naturalist* by Seamus Heaney, Faber and Faber Ltd, 1966. Permission sought.

Toni Morrison, 'Eve Remembering': from *Five Poems* by Toni Morrison with silhouettes by Kara E. Walker, Rainmaker Editions, 2002. Permission sought.

Edwin Muir, 'One Foot in Eden Still, I Stand': from *Collected Poems* by Edwin Muir, Faber and Faber Ltd, 1960.

Saunders Lewis, 'To the Good Thief': reprinted by kind permission of Siwan Jones.

Ann Griffiths, 'I Saw Him Standing': English translation reproduced by kind permission of Rowan Williams.

Malcolm Guite, 'O Sapientia': from *Sounding the Seasons* © Malcolm Guite, 2015. Published by Canterbury Press. Used by permission. rights@hymnsam.co.uk

Emily Dickinson, 'This World Is Not Conclusion': from *The Poems of Emily Dickinson: Reading Edition*, edited by Ralph W. Franklin, Cambridge, Mass.: The Belknap Press of Harvard University Press, Copyright © 1998, 1999 by the President and Fellows of Harvard College. Copyright © 1951, 1955 by the President and Fellows of Harvard College. Copyright © renewed 1979, 1983 by the President and Fellows of Harvard College. Copyright © 1914, 1918, 1919, 1924, 1929, 1930, 1932, 1935, 1937, 1942 by Martha Dickinson Bianchi.

Acknowledgements

Copyright © 1952, 1957, 1958, 1963, 1965 by Mary L. Hampson. Used by permission. All rights reserved.

T. S. Eliot, 'Little Gidding' (extract): from *Four Quartets* by T. S. Eliot, Faber and Faber Ltd, 1942.

Roger McGough, 'The Father, the Son': from *Collected Poems* by Roger McGough, Viking, 2003. Permission sought.

Piers Plowright, 'Signs': reproduced by kind permission of Dr Poh Sim Plowright.

Khadijah Ibrahiim, 'When My Time Come': from *Another Crossing* (Peepal Tree Press, 2014) © Khadijah Ibrahiim, reproduced by permission of Peepal Tree Press.

Every effort has been made to acknowledge fully the sources of material reproduced in this book. The publisher apologizes for any omissions that may remain and, if notified, will ensure that full acknowledgements are made in a subsequent edition.

Introduction

This book begins with four poems to reflect on during the four days from Ash Wednesday to the first Sunday in Lent. The rest of the content is then divided into six groups of six poems each for the weeks leading up to and including Holy Week. It finishes with a final section of ten poems for Easter and our new life in Christ. The book has been designed to reflect every age of English poetry and I have, therefore, with some reluctance, had to limit myself to one poem per poet.

Although a devotional book, this is not a book of devotional poetry. It encompasses a wide range of subjects, both human and divine. As Austin Farrer once wrote:

Faith perishes if it is walled in or confined. If it is anywhere, it must be everywhere, like God himself: if God is in your life, he is in all things, for he is God. You must be able to spread the area of your recognition for him and the basis of your conviction about him, as widely as your thought will range.[1]

That is a very carefully balanced statement. It does not suggest that, say, a poem about trees is a separate source of revelation. The light that we see with has been given in Jesus and our eyes have been opened by the Holy Spirit, so if we look at the world in that light and see with those eyes, we will be able to see something of God everywhere. As Farrer says, if our faith is not to be walled in, we must be able to spread the area of our recognition of God as widely as our mind and imagination will range. In particular, I hope that people will be able to do that in relation to these poems.

Each poem is followed by a short piece on the writer and a brief analysis of the poem. I have not often sought to draw out moral or theological lessons, as I believe that the point about poems is that they speak for themselves. That is why a poem is a poem and not a piece of prose, and why each of these poems offers insights that can lead the reader deeper into the mystery of Christ crucified and risen.

ASH WEDNESDAY
TO LENT 1
WEEK 1
PREPARATION

Ash Wednesday
Surview

Thomas Hardy

'Cogitavi vias meas'

A cry from the green-grained sticks of the fire
    Made me gaze where it seemed to be:
'Twas my own voice talking therefrom to me
On how I had walked when my sun was higher –
    My heart in its arrogancy.

'You held not to whatsoever was true,'
    Said my own voice talking to me:
'Whatsoever was just you were slack to see;
Kept not things lovely and pure in view,'
    Said my own voice talking to me.

'You slighted her that endureth all,'
    Said my own voice talking to me;
'Vaunteth not, trusteth hopefully;
That suffereth long and is kind withal,'
    Said my own voice talking to me.

'You taught not that which you set about,'
    Said my own voice talking to me;
'That the greatest of things is Charity . . . '
– And the sticks burnt low, and the fire went out,
    And my voice ceased talking to me.

Thomas Hardy (1840–1928)

As a teenager, I was captivated by the major novels of Thomas Hardy. Their themes of love and suffering, poverty and ill fortune are direct and moving, as shown by the number of film and TV adaptations the novels have inspired. Like others, I became conscious of the hostile supernatural power that looms behind the course of events in Hardy's books. It was later that I discovered Hardy's poetry and realized that he was a major poet as well as a great novelist. Indeed, although Hardy first acquired fame as a novelist, he thought of himself first of all as a poet, and his poetry has been increasingly appreciated by discriminating critics from the time it was first published until the present day.

Hardy's father was a stonemason. Despite the poverty of his background, Thomas was able to train as an architect and specialize in church architecture. It is clear that, to the end of his life, Hardy could not reconcile the suffering of the world with belief in a loving power behind the universe, and he came to think that any power was of an impersonal kind. Religious belief, however, had gone deep into him from his Anglican childhood. He never ceased to love the Church and attend its services. He loved its music and architecture. Indeed, at the age of 18, he was attracted to Evangelicalism and even had a dream of being ordained.

Hardy's torn feelings about religion and his ambivalence about belief are reflected in 'The darkling thrush'. We will all have had one of those days when life seems utterly bleak and desolate. I can never forget those late November afternoons away at boarding school when, at dusk, I would look out over empty playing fields and sense the gloom settle in like the cold fog. In the first verse of this poem, Hardy describes such a day. He is leaning on a gate on a frosty, grey day in winter, looking out at the countryside. All seems broken, reduced to nothing and desolate, and sensible people have gone home to huddle round a fire.

Then he hears a bird singing, an old thrush 'frail, gaunt, and small, in blast-beruffled plume'.

4

That I could think there trembled through
   His happy good-night air
Some blessed Hope, whereof he knew
   And I was unaware.

It is noticeable that 'Hope' is spelt with a capital 'H'. Despite the terrible suffering in the world, to which Hardy was so sensitive; despite his own failings in love, of which he was highly aware; despite the findings of Darwin, which seemed to reveal only the impersonal force of evolution driving life forwards, something still haunted him; some inkling that there could be an ultimate good behind it all. He was not aware of it, but the joyful sound of the thrush flinging his soul on the growing gloom seemed a witness to some sublime beauty.

For this book, however, I have chosen 'Surview'.

Hardy married Emma Gifford in 1874. Sadly, it was not a happy marriage, and when she died in 1912, he was haunted by her, revisiting the places associated with their courtship. It was then also that he started writing poems that reflected his grief and remorse. Then, two years later, he married his secretary Florence Dugdale, who was 39 years younger than he was. He was still preoccupied with feelings about his first wife, however.

In this poem, he is looking into the fire when he begins an inner dialogue. He finds himself stricken by the wonderful words of 1 Corinthians 13, especially Paul's theme that what matters above everything is love and without love nothing is of worth. The words before the poem in Latin, Cogitavi vias meas, are from Psalm 119.59. In the Book of Common Prayer, which Hardy would have used, they are translated, 'I called my own ways to remembrance'.

Thinking particularly about his two wives in relation to Paul's theme in 1 Corinthians, he is pained by how far he has fallen short of that divine charity.

Thursday
King Lear (Act III, Scene IV)
William Shakespeare

LEAR   Prithee, go in thyself: seek thine own ease:
    This tempest will not give me leave to ponder
    On things would hurt me more. But I'll go in.
    To the Fool
    In, boy; go first. You houseless poverty, –
    Nay, get thee in. I'll pray, and then I'll sleep.
    Fool goes in
    Poor naked wretches, whereso'er you are,
    That bide the pelting of this pitiless storm,
    How shall your houseless heads and unfed sides,
    Your loop'd and window'd raggedness, defend you
    From seasons such as these? O, I have ta'en
    Too little care of this! Take physic, pomp;
    Expose thyself to feel what wretches feel,
    That thou mayst shake the superflux to them,
    And show the heavens more just.

William Shakespeare (1564–1616)

Whether Shakespeare was a Catholic, Protestant or agnostic is end-lessly argued over. One thing is certain, he knew the Scriptures. There are 1,350 references to the Bible in his work. As Ulrich Simon wrote:

It is enough to say firmly that Shakespeare writes and produces tragedies in a Christian world with a Christian past and present.

Baptised, married and buried in the Church of England, he lives and speaks within the resonance of the Bishop's Bible and the Prayer Book.[2]

In this great play, King Lear wants to hand over his kingdom to his daughters, but is desperate for their love and pushes them to say how much they love him. Goneril and Regan go along with this and assure him of unlimited love. Cordelia gives him a sincere response that she would love her husband even more than her father. Lear, furious at this, rejects her. Then he, having given up his power, finds himself at the mercy of Goneril and Regan, and they, finding him a burden, treat him with more and more disdain. Eventually, after a series of tragedies, Lear finds himself alone with his fool on a wild heath in a fierce storm. For the first time in his life, he thinks of the homeless and starving, of whom there were many in England at the time. He thinks of them, like him, caught in the storm, with nothing to protect them. He is stricken by remorse: 'O, I have ta'en too little care of this!' He knows that his pride needs to take a painful medicine, that he needs to feel what wretches feel. By this he hopes to shake the extravagant surplus on which he has lived into the lives of those who need it 'and show the heavens more just'.

The Church has often talked about sex – far too much – when what it ought to have talked about is power. As Shakespeare knew, power is far more dangerous to humanity than sex. We should not think of power only in terms of the powerful. Very few human relationships are based on a genuine equality; most reflect some disparity of power. Those who are the most powerful have a dreadful capacity to be blind to this. It is only when, as in sexual abuse cases, there is a public scandal that we see how one person in power can manipulate another. Poor Lear was blind to the fact that if he were to hand over his power to his daughters, he would literally be in their power, and, sadly, two of them went on to exploit this and make him feel like dirt. It was only on the heath in the storm that he realized this truth, once that he was totally powerless.

At the heart of the Christian faith is the message that God has become powerless for our sake. The God behind the universe became nothing that he might win our allegiance not by coercion, explicit or implicit, but by our simple recognition that he is totally for us. This is a truth sublimely expressed in the early Christian hymn in Philippians 2, and which St Paul expounded on so powerfully in the second chapter of his letter to the Corinthians. Perhaps something of this awareness lies behind Shakespeare's insight into Lear's situation here.

Friday
The poor parson

Geoffrey Chaucer

A good man was there of religion,
He was a poor COUNTRY PARSON,
But rich he was in holy thought and work.
He was a learned man also, a clerk,
Who Christ's own gospel truly sought to preach;
Devoutly his parishioners would he teach.
Gracious he was and wondrously diligent,
Patient in adversity and well content,
Many times thus proven had he [been].
He excommunicated not to force a fee,
But rather would he give, there is no doubt,
Unto his poor parishioners about,
Some of his income, even of his property.
He could in little find sufficiency.
Wide was his parish, houses far asunder,
But never did he fail, for rain or thunder,
In sickness, or in sin, or any state,
To visit the farthest, regardless their financial state,
Going by foot, and in his hand, a stave.
This fine example to his flock he gave,
That first he wrought and afterwards he taught;
Out of the gospel then that text he caught,
And this metaphor he added thereunto –
That, if gold would rust, what shall iron do?
For if the priest be foul, in whom we trust,

No wonder that a layman thinks of lust?
And shame it is, if priest take thought for keep,
A shitty shepherd, looking after clean sheep.
A truly good example a priest should give,
Is his own chastity, how his flock should live.
He never let his benefice for hire,
And leave his sheep encumbered in the mire,
And ran to London, up to old Saint Paul's
To get himself a chantry there for souls,
Nor in some fraternity did he withhold;
But dwelt at home and kept so well the fold
That never wolf could make his plans miscarry;
He was a shepherd and not mercenary.
And holy though he was, and virtuous,
To sinners he was not impiteous,
Nor haughty in his speech, nor too divine,
But in all teaching courteous and benign.
To lead folk into Heaven by means of gentleness
By good example was his business.
But if some sinful one proved obstinate,
Whoever, of high or low financial state,
He put to sharp rebuke, to say the least.
I think there never was a better priest.
He had no thirst for pomp or ceremony,
Nor spiced his conscience and morality,
But Christ's own law, and His apostles' twelve
He taught, but first he followed it himself.

Geoffrey Chaucer (c.1340s–1400)

The fourteenth century was a tumultuous time, with the black death killing between 40 and 60 per cent of England's population of 6 million. Chaucer had direct experience of this, as his family inherited money from relatives who had died of the plague. Under the

Plantagenet kings Edward III and Richard II, it was also the time of the Hundred Years War, fought in part to decide which royal family should rule large tracts of France. Yet it was also a period of great mystical writers, such as Julian of Norwich and the anonymous author of *The Cloud of Unknowing*.

No less amazing is that it included Geoffrey Chaucer and his cheerful, ribald stories, as told by pilgrims on their way to Canterbury. Regarded as the father of English poetry, Chaucer firmed up the writing of Middle English at a time when literature was mainly in Latin or French. Writing in lines with five stresses in rhyming couplets, he wrote poetry that has been admired in every age. He did this while earning a living as a civil servant, courtier, diplomat and member of Parliament. He was the first poet to be buried in what is now Poets' Corner in Westminster Abbey.

In *The Canterbury Tales*, Chaucer depicts the Church at its most venal and hypocritical. He was a serious Christian believer, however, and in 'The parson's tale', the last of the tales in the book, he set out the ideal for what a Christian priest should be. He wrote in *The Canterbury Tales*, 'Now I beg all those that listen to this little treatise, or read it, that if there be anything in it that pleases them, they thank our Lord Jesus Christ for it, from whom proceeds all understanding and goodness.'

Many centuries later, another poet, George Herbert, would set out his ideal of how a country priest should conduct his ministry, but the essentials of what Herbert laid out are already there in this wonderful portrait given by Chaucer. As he knew real-life examples of all the church officials he satirized in his tales, it is legitimate for us to surmise that he also knew real-life examples of the poor parson in this story.

The word 'parson' comes from 'person' – in Latin, *persona ecclesiasticae*. The parson is a person in the sense that he represents in his person – he personifies – the Christian community for which he (or now, she) has responsibility. The word is not much used now but was a standard term in the Middle Ages.

In the poem, the parson is well educated and devout, using his education to teach his parishioners. He does this graciously and tirelessly. He has a modest lifestyle, not seeking to make money but giving it away when he can. He visits people on foot whatever the weather or their financial state. He knows that unless he sets a good example, he cannot expect better from his flock. Drawing on the biblical image of Jesus, 'I am the good shepherd', he tries to be just that. He does not run away to a more lucrative post in the city but stays with his flock. If people need to be rebuked, he does this, even if they are people of status. Above all, he seeks to minister by gentleness and good example.

Saturday
Lachrimae amantis
Geoffrey Hill

What is there in my heart that you should sue
so fiercely for its love? What kind of care
brings you as though a stranger to my door
through the long night and in the icy dew
seeking the heart that will not harbour you,
that keeps itself religiously secure?
At this dark solstice filled with frost and fire
your passion's ancient wounds must bleed anew.
So many nights the angel of my house
has fed such urgent comfort through a dream,
whispered 'your lord is coming, he is close'
that I have drowsed half-faithful for a time
bathed in pure tones of promise and remorse:
'tomorrow I shall wake to welcome him.'

Geoffrey Hill (1932–2016)

Geoffrey Hill was born and brought up in Worcestershire, and that part of the world always meant much to him, as expressed in his poems about its ancient kingdom of Mercia. When quite young, he composed poetry as he went on solitary walks and he was first published while a student at Oxford University. For most of his career, he was Professor of Poetry at Leeds, before taking up other distinguished academic positions, including being Professor of Poetry at Oxford. He won many awards. In 2013, he was described as the greatest poet in the English language. His poetry is notoriously difficult, and his

13

criticism notoriously polemical, with its prophetic anger at the ills of modern culture. Even as a student, he defended the right of poets to be difficult in order to counter the easy simplifications of the age, such simplifications being the tool of tyrants. There is also a battle in his poetry between the lyricism for which he had a gift, and which beautifies, and the truth he was committed to tell, which was often brutal. In contrast to the prevailing outlook of the time, he was a serious Christian, and his second wife was a Christian priest.

This lovely poem is surprisingly accessible. It begins with a question: what is there about me that God should care so much; that he should be like a lover on his knees pleading for a 'yes'? This pleading is so intense it can be described as 'fierce'. You can almost see the passion in the lover's face and eyes.

> What is there in my heart that you should sue so fiercely for
> its love?

This God comes to us as a stranger at the door after a long hard journey.

> What kind of care
> brings you as though a stranger to my door
> through the long night and in the icy dew?

For the Christian reader, the words cannot help but bring to mind the parables of the lost sheep and the lost coin. God is like a shepherd who searches through the mountains to find the one sheep that is lost, or the woman who scrabbles all over the floor looking for her lost coin. God never gives us up on us, but searches us out wherever we may hide. This was the pattern of Jesus' own ministry to those on the margins of the society of his day, and he made it clear that this is but a human working out of God's eternal searching for every human soul. So the stranger who treks through the long night and the icy dew is, in fact, the eternal Son of God making the incredible journey of self-limitation in the Incarnation.

The second verse reveals an acute self-knowledge in recognizing that religion can be a kind of security that keeps God at a distance. We know that there is something in us that will not harbour God, that does not want to let him in and, moreover, can sometimes use religion as a way to keep him out; the heart can keep itself 'religiously secure'. Despite this, God keeps coming, though again the poet recognizes his own ambivalence. He knows he is only half-faithful and, though he is full of remorse, he puts off the encounter with a promise to welcome God in the morning: 'Tomorrow I shall wake to welcome him.' Genuine religion, as expressed in this poem, is based not only on the belief that God goes on seeking us out but also on honest self-knowledge.

WEEK 1
TESTING

Monday

Batter my heart, three person'd God, Holy Sonnet 14

John Donne

Batter my heart, three-person'd God, for you
As yet but knock, breathe, shine, and seek to mend;
That I may rise, and stand, o'erthrow me, and bend
Your force to break, blow, burn, and make me new.
I, like an usurped town, to another due,
Labour to admit you, but Oh, to no end.
Reason, your viceroy in me, me should defend,
But is captived, and proves weak or untrue.
Yet dearly I love you, and would be loved fain,
But am betrothed unto your enemy:
Divorce me, untie or break that knot again,
Take me to you, imprison me, for I,
Except you enthrall me, never shall be free,
Nor ever chaste, except you ravish me.

John Donne (1572–1631)

John Donne was a man of strong passions. He had a reputation as a rake in his younger days, and this is reflected in his love poetry. It is regarded as the finest in the English language. How far these poems are based on actual experience and how far they come out of his imagination is not known. As a young man, he travelled in Italy and Spain. He was also ambitious and was poised to rise high in what was, in effect, the civil service. Born a Roman Catholic, he became a member of the Church of England and, indeed, if he had not changed his allegiance, he would not have been able to be so employed. This switch made him feel uneasy to the end of his days.

In 1601, he secretly married a young heiress, Anne More, without her parent's permission. When this was discovered, he lost his job and they lived in penury in the country with a rapidly expanding family of children – 12 in the end. A number died young and Donne remarked that, though it made one less mouth to feed, he could not afford the burial expenses.

In 1615, he was ordained, not because he had any particular desire to be but because King James ordered it. Once ordained, he took his religious commitment seriously and this is reflected in his 'Holy Sonnets' and his sermons. When he became Dean of St Paul's in 1621, this gave ample scope for his oratory, and his sermons have become regarded as among the finest of all time. T. S. Eliot, before he was baptized, was drawn to the Christian faith by the literary qualities of Donne's sermons and those of Lancelot Andrewes. Indeed, Eliot was responsible for the re-evaluation of Donne after two centuries of neglect. Eliot later came to prefer the sermons of Andrewes, writing about Donne that 'there hangs the shadow of the impure motive'. Donne was indeed something of a showman. He loved the theatre and it was the age of Shakespeare. He had a vivid imagination as well as strong emotions, so perhaps not surprisingly his sermons are nothing if not dramatic.

W. B. Yeats once wrote, 'We make out of the quarrel with others, rhetoric, and out of the quarrel with ourselves, poetry.' This applies even more to Donne than it does to Yeats himself. In his love poetry, he is arguing with women and in his religious poetry he is arguing with God. In this poem, however, he is not so much arguing as confronting God in order to force him to act. It is a poem in which all Donne's passion is present, expressed in strong, violent imagery. He wants God to batter his heart like a battering ram and complains that, up to now, he has been too gentle. Then the imagery becomes that of a wrestling match. He wants God to overthrow and break him. Even more, he wants God to blow and burn on him as though he were a piece of metal being heated in the fire of a forge so that something new can be fashioned.

Like St Augustine, Donne knows that he cannot do anything himself. He is inside a captured town. Like St Paul, he knows that he is a divided self. His reason should be able to guide him but this too has been captured. Then comes a moment of helpless humility. At the heart of all the turbulence, he wants simply to say, 'Dearly I love you, and would be loved fain.' But even that is not enough, because he is engaged to God's enemy. So God himself will have to divorce him and break that bond. Unless God imprisons and enthrals him, he will never be free. In a final bold image, he knows his sexual drive is so strong that he can never be chaste unless God himself overwhelms and 'ravishes' him.

Not all of us have such strong emotions as John Donne, and we are all different. It would be a strange person, though, who never experienced any inner conflict; some tussle between what the best side wants and what the senses or ego drive us to. What Donne suggests is that we bring this conflict before God himself and have it out with him.

Tuesday

God moves in a mysterious way

William Cowper

God moves in a mysterious way,
    His wonders to perform;
He plants his footsteps in the sea,
    And rides upon the storm.

Deep in unfathomable mines
    Of never-failing skill;
He treasures up his bright designs,
    And works His sovereign will.

Ye fearful saints fresh courage take,
    The clouds ye so much dread
Are big with mercy, and shall break
    In blessings on your head.

Judge not the Lord by feeble sense,
    But trust him for his grace;
Behind a frowning providence,
    He hides a smiling face.

His purposes will ripen fast,
    Unfolding ev'ry hour;
The bud may have a bitter taste,
    But sweet will be the flow'r.

Blind unbelief is sure to err,
  And scan his work in vain;
God is his own interpreter,
  And he will make it plain.

William Cowper (1731–1800)

Cowper was the son of a clergyman whose family and that of his mother were well connected she with the poet John Donne. Cowper's mother died when he was six and he was bullied at school – both major causes of the depression that was to afflict his whole life. He had a good education at Westminster School and, later in life, made much admired poetic translations of the great Latin and Greek classics. He qualified as a barrister but the law did not interest him. Offered a lucrative job in the House of Lords, he had first to undergo a public examination. The thought of this so threw him that he had the first of his many breakdowns and was committed to a mental institution in St Albans. Recovering, he went to live with the Revd Morley Unwin and his wife Mary. When Morley died, he lived with Mary, moving to Olney in Buckinghamshire. She devotedly cared for him and, later in life, he cared for her when she was dying.

When he was at Olney, he met the slave-trader-turned-abolitionist John Newton. He lent his support to the abolitionist movement and with Newton produced *The Olney Hymnbook*, which contains a number of hymns that have been popular ever since – the one quoted here being one of them.

Cowper was the most popular poet of his time, and his poetry has been admired by discriminating critics ever since. Despite this and despite the fact that he had good friendships with both men and women, he continued to suffer from crippling depression. This took a particularly sad and terrible form: although he had experienced an orthodox evangelical conversion, he believed that he was eternally damned. A number of times he was very close to committing suicide. What somehow kept him going was living a quiet life in the country, playing with his favourite pets, such as a hare, and writing poetry – the very process of articulating his plight in verse had a therapeutic effect.

One of Cowper's friendships was with the strong, vivacious Lady Austen. They quarrelled bitterly when he rejected her veiled proposal of marriage, but not before she inspired him to write, in one night, *The Diverting History of John Gilpin*, which was spectacularly successful from the start for its fun and humour. This light-heartedness, however, was a desperate cover for the experiences of suffering and isolation that the poem describes. In a poem called 'The stricken deer', Cowper likens himself to a deer that has been pierced by arrows and left alone to die, finding comfort alongside another that has been pierced, Christ himself.

> I was a stricken deer, that left the herd
> Long since; with many an arrow deep infixt
> My panting side was charg'd, when I withdrew
> To seek a tranquil death in distant shades.
> There was I found by one who had himself
> Been hurt by th' archers. In his side he bore,
> And in his hands and feet, the cruel scars.
> With gentle force soliciting the darts,
> He drew them forth, and heal'd, and bade me live.

In another poem, 'The castaway', Cowper tells the story of a man drowning after his boat was caught in a storm and then compares that to his own predicament.

> No voice divine the storm allay'd,
>   No light propitious shone;
> When, snatch'd from all effectual aid,
>   We perish'd, each alone:

But I beneath a rougher sea,
And whelm'd in deeper gulfs than he.

These terrible depressions are the dark clouds mentioned in the hymn. Despite them, Cowper sought to put his trust in God. Although he could not understand the meaning of all he had been through, he trusted that God would have a good purpose and that behind the frowning providence there was a smiling face.

Wednesday
Twice

Christina Rossetti

I took my heart in my hand
(O my love, O my love),
I said: Let me fall or stand,
Let me live or die,
But this once hear me speak –
(O my love, O my love) –
Yet a woman's words are weak;
You should speak, not I.

You took my heart in your hand
With a friendly smile,
With a critical eye you scanned,
Then set it down,
And said: It is still unripe,
Better wait a while;
Wait while the skylarks pipe,
Till the corn grows brown

As you set it down it broke –
Broke, but I did not wince;
I smiled at the speech you spoke,
At your judgment that I heard:
But I have not often smiled
Since then, nor questioned since,

Nor cared for corn-flowers wild,
Nor sung with the singing bird.

I take my heart in my hand,
O my God, O my God,
My broken heart in my hand:
Thou hast seen, judge Thou
My hope was written on sand,
O my God, O my God:
Now let Thy judgment stand –
Yea, judge me now

This contemned of a man,
This marred one heedless day,
This heart take Thou to scan
Both within and without:
Refine with fire its gold,
Purge Thou its dross away –
Yea, hold it in Thy hold,
Whence none can pluck it out.

I take my heart in my hand –
I shall not die, but live –
Before Thy face I stand;
I, for Thou callest such:
All that I have I bring,
All that I am I give,
Smile Thou and I shall sing,
But shall not question much.

Christina Rossetti (1830–1894)

Christina Rossetti was born into a highly talented family, her brother
being the influential painter Dante Gabriel Rossetti, who painted

her portrait a number of times. She had a wide and deep education at home from her parents in a house in Bloomsbury that was full of poets, revolutionaries and members of the Pre-Raphaelite brotherhood, her father being a political exile from Italy. This happy childhood came to an end when, in her teens, her father became seriously ill, with the added prospect of going blind. He had to give up his teaching at King's College, London, and went into a severe depression before dying 11 years later. The family became very poor and Christina herself had a breakdown: one of a number. She rejected three suitors, mainly on the grounds that they did not share the Anglo-Catholic faith that was fundamental to her life and art.

She started writing poetry as soon as she could write, was published early and achieved great popular and critical success with a book of poems when she was 31. She has been an influence on other poets up to the present day. Her importance was again emphasized in the 1970s when critics went beyond the themes of her poetry to admire the skill and subtlety of her versification. She wrote in many forms, and is the author of two of the best-loved Christmas carols – 'In the bleak midwinter' and 'Love came down at Christmas'. She is honoured in the Church of England on 27 April.

For 11 years, Christina Rossetti worked as a volunteer at St Mary Magdalene's House of Charity in Highgate for former prostitutes. The poem above concerns a woman who has been treated badly by a man. She gave her heart to him and, no doubt, her body as well, but he found her 'unripe' and broke her heart, sending her into a state of dejection in which she could no longer appreciate the beauty of the natural world. Then, a second time she gave her heart, this time a broken heart, hence the title 'Twice', but this time it was God to whom she gave it. This love would not just purify her but also hold her secure: 'I shall not die but live' (see Psalm 118.17).

The woman feels that she is called as the person she is and will give herself this second time in words that echo the vows of the wedding service. She looks for God's smile so that she can sing without questioning him.

    I, for Thou callest such:
    All that I have I bring,
    All that I am I give,
    Smile Thou and I shall sing,
    But shall not question much.

Thursday

The Rime of the Ancient Mariner, (Part IV)

Samuel Taylor Coleridge

Alone, alone, all, all alone,
Alone on a wide wide sea!
And never a saint took pity on
My soul in agony.

The many men, so beautiful!
And they all dead did lie:
And a thousand thousand slimy things
Lived on; and so did I.

I looked upon the rotting sea,
And drew my eyes away;
I looked upon the rotting deck,
And there the dead men lay.

I looked to heaven, and tried to pray;
But or ever a prayer had gusht,
A wicked whisper came, and made
My heart as dry as dust . . .

Beyond the shadow of the ship,
I watched the water-snakes:
They moved in tracks of shining white,

And when they reared, the elfish light
Fell off in hoary flakes.

Within the shadow of the ship
I watched their rich attire:
Blue, glossy green, and velvet black,
They coiled and swam; and every track
Was a flash of golden fire.

O happy living things! no tongue
Their beauty might declare:
A spring of love gushed from my heart,
And I blessed them unaware:
Sure my kind saint took pity on me,
And I blessed them unaware.

The self-same moment I could pray;
And from my neck so free
The Albatross fell off, and sank
Like lead into the sea.

Samuel Taylor Coleridge (1772–1834)

Coleridge had a good education and read widely from a young age.
He showed signs of instability at Cambridge, however, when he ran
away to join the army under an assumed name, from which he had to
be rescued by his family. He suffered from physical ailments and de-
pression, for which he took laudanum (opium), to which he became
seriously addicted. This was one factor in his unhappy marriage,
leading to a split from his wife, and also a quarrel with Wordsworth.
It has been speculated that he was bipolar. Despite this instability,
he was one of the most talented of the English poets, and a hugely
influential literary critic up to our own day. T. S. Eliot wrote that he
was 'perhaps the greatest of English critics, and in a sense the last'.

He joined with the poet Robert Southey to found a utopian society, a Pantisocracy, in Pennsylvania but it did not come to fruition.

He and Wordsworth published *Lyrical Ballads* in 1798, with poems mainly by Wordsworth, but which also contained *The Rime of the Ancient Mariner*. This book is thought of as marking the beginnings of the Romantic movement. One distinctive contribution Coleridge made to this movement was his stress on the role of the imagination. He thought there was a primary imagination in God, which is repeated in human consciousness, and our works of imagination are echoes of this. There had to be a 'suspension of disbelief' for this divine faculty to operate. His best-known works, 'Kubla Kahn' and the poem above, certainly bear out the description of him as imaginative.

Coleridge was influenced by German idealism, which is based on the belief that what really matters are the ideas of the mind, not things in themselves. This philosophy elided in his mind with Platonism, with its similar emphasis on the reality of abstract ideas such as beauty, truth and goodness. At one time, Coleridge was a preacher in a Unitarian church and nearly became ordained, but he returned to the Church of England, in which his father had been a much respected priest and headmaster.

In the poem quoted above, an ancient mariner feels compelled to tell his story to others. He describes how, on a voyage, his ship was driven far south in the Atlantic, but was led out of trouble by an albatross. The mariner had shot the albatross, after which the ship got into great difficulties and the sailors hung the albatross round the mariner's neck. They passed a ghost ship, after which the sailors died one by one. The mariner, left alone in agony, tries and fails to pray. Then he sees the sea snakes in the sea. Once they revolted him but now he is struck both by their sheer liveliness and their beauty. The albatross falls off his neck and he can pray. The poem goes on to say that when the mariner got back to port, he was compelled for ever to tell his story to others, that it might teach them:

Thursday

He prayeth best, who loveth best
All things both great and small;
For the dear God who loveth us,
He made and loveth all.

The person who has been listening to him goes away 'a sadder and a wiser man'.

Friday
In Memoriam

Alfred, Lord Tennyson

Strong Son of God, immortal Love,
    Whom we, that have not seen thy face,
    By faith, and faith alone, embrace,
Believing where we cannot prove;

Thine are these orbs of light and shade;
    Thou madest Life in man and brute;
    Thou madest Death; and lo, thy foot
Is on the skull which thou hast made.

Thou wilt not leave us in the dust:
    Thou madest man, he knows not why,
    He thinks he was not made to die;
And thou hast made him: thou art just.

Thou seemest human and divine,
    The highest, holiest manhood, thou.
    Our wills are ours, we know not how,
Our wills are ours, to make them thine.

Our little systems have their day;
    They have their day and cease to be:
    They are but broken lights of thee,
And thou, O Lord, art more than they.

We have but faith: we cannot know;
    For knowledge is of things we see;
    And yet we trust it comes from thee,
A beam in darkness: let it grow.

Let knowledge grow from more to more,
    But more of reverence in us dwell;
    That mind and soul, according well,
May make one music as before,

But vaster. We are fools and slight;
    We mock thee when we do not fear:
    But help thy foolish ones to bear;
Help thy vain worlds to bear thy light.

Forgive what seem'd my sin in me,
    What seem'd my worth since I began;
    For merit lives from man to man,
And not from man, O Lord, to thee.

Forgive my grief for one removed,
    Thy creature, whom I found so fair.
    I trust he lives in thee, and there
I find him worthier to be loved.

Forgive these wild and wandering cries,
    Confusions of a wasted youth;
    Forgive them where they fail in truth,
And in thy wisdom make me wise.

Alfred, Lord Tennyson (1809–1892)

Tennyson was the son of a highly talented Lincolnshire clergyman,
who took personal care of the education of his many children. He

wrote poetry from a young age, won a major prize at Cambridge for one of his poems and had his first book of verse published when he was 21. When his father died, he had to leave Cambridge without a degree to look after his family. Then, when they had to leave the rectory, Tennyson moved to London, where an unwise investment meant that he had to live modestly. His second book of poems met with hostile reviews and this so discouraged him that he did not publish again for ten years, though he continued to write. His reputation recovered to the extent that he became Poet Laureate, and was twice offered a peerage – first by Disraeli, which he turned down, and then by Gladstone, who pleaded with him to accept it. A good number of his phrases have entered the English language. He is the ninth most frequently quoted writer in the *Oxford Dictionary of Quotations*.

At Cambridge, he became close friends with Arthur Hallam, so when Hallam died of a stroke at the age of 22, Tennyson was devastated. The above is a long poem in memory of Hallam. It is really 130 poems, each one of which has many verses. They explore all Tennyson's feelings of grief and loss, and struggle to believe in God. Queen Victoria said that she found great comfort in reading it. T. S. Eliot, like many others, much admired Tennyson's mastery of verse, saying that he had the finest ear of any poet since Milton. He also regarded *In Memoriam* as a great religious poem, but for a different reason from that of Tennyson's contemporaries: 'It is not religious because of the quality of its faith, but because of the quality of its doubt. Its faith is a poor thing but its doubt is a very intense experience. *In Memoriam* is a poem of despair, but of despair of a religious kind.'³ The verses quoted above provide the preface to the poem as a whole. They reveal the poet desperately trying to hold on to faith as he faces his terrible loss.

Saturday
In memory of W. B. Yeats

W. H. Auden

III
Earth, receive an honoured guest:
William Yeats is laid to rest.
Let the Irish vessel lie
Emptied of its poetry.
In the nightmare of the dark
All the dogs of Europe bark,
And the living nations wait,
Each sequestered in its hate;
Intellectual disgrace
Stares from every human face,
And the seas of pity lie
Locked and frozen in each eye.
Follow, poet, follow right
To the bottom of the night,
With your unconstraining voice
Still persuade us to rejoice;
With the farming of a verse
Make a vineyard of the curse,
Sing of human unsuccess
In a rapture of distress;
In the deserts of the heart
Let the healing fountain start,
In the prison of his days
Teach the free man how to praise.

W. H. Auden (1907–1973)

Auden was probably the most naturally talented poet of the twentieth century, with a verbal dexterity that approached wizardry. His poetry was acclaimed from its first publication and, for many, he was the voice of the 1930s.

About 1940, he returned to the faith that he had abandoned as a teenager to pursue the delights of the flesh. This faith suffused all his later poetry, even though nearly all of it is on secular subjects. If T. S. Eliot is a poet of the *via negativa*, Auden is a poet of the *via positiva*, for he is able to delight in and offer praise for the tiniest details and most mundane features of creation.

Yeats, who died in 1939, was the major poet of an earlier generation, 40 years before Auden and 20 years before Eliot – a towering figure for all poets who followed him. The years 1939, when Yeats died, and 1940, when Auden wrote this poem in his honour, were a very dark time. In another poem, 'September 1, 1939', Auden called the 1930s a 'low dishonest decade', and, in 1940, the prospect for Britain against the power of the Nazis looked very grim indeed. This is reflected in the second and third verses. The nations of Europe are sequestered in their hate; all that led up to this was an intellectual disgrace and now all pity is frozen.

It is just at this very dark time, however, that the poet is called to go into that darkness and, still with unconstraining voice, persuade us to rejoice. The fifth verse is based, very cleverly, on the myth of the fall in the book of Genesis. There, the fact that we have to labour on the land and toil for a living is regarded as part of the punishment, the curse, for Adam's disobedience. Despite this, the careful crafting of the poem, his farming, can make something wonderful of the earth: a vineyard or a poem. So, finally, in the deserts of our personal lives, the poet can act as a healing fountain. We may be imprisoned, but we are still free in our minds and can learn to praise.[4]

WEEK 2
GRACE

Monday
I count the moments of my mercies up

Elizabeth Jennings

I count the moments of my mercies up.
I make a list of love and find it full.
I do all this before I fall asleep.

Others examine consciences. I tell
My beads of gracious moments shining still.
I count my good hours and they guide me well

Into a sleepless night. It's when I fill
Pages with what I think I am made for,
A life of writing poems. Then may they heal

The pain of silence for all those who stare
At stars as I do but are helpless to
Make the bright necklace. May I set ajar

The door of closed minds. Words come and words go
And poetry is pain as well as passion.
But in the large flights of imagination

I see for one crammed second, order so
Explicit that I need no more persuasion.

Elizabeth Jennings (1926–2001)

Elizabeth Jennings was born and brought up in Oxford, where she remained all her life. She had a good education and studied at St Anne's College, Oxford. At the age of 13, she discovered a gift for poetry and, at the same time, became a lifelong, consciously devout Roman Catholic. She was the only woman member of the new group of poets in the 1950s known as The Movement and, according to Michael Schmidt, was 'the most universally loved poet of her generation'.[5] She won a number of prizes.

Elizabeth Jennings was sensitive and mentally fragile. She had a number of breakdowns and spent time in the vast mental hospitals of the time, about which she wrote some moving poems. In her poetry, we see her working her way through the temptation to be sorry for herself to a growing appreciation of other people and the world around her. The themes of her poems are ones of grace, thankfulness and praise.

In the above poem, a number of ideas central to her poetry come together: gracious moments, and appreciation and gratitude for them; her vocation as a poet and the imagination that makes this possible. It is important to stress that, for her, it was a disciplined imagination. The order she sees as so explicit in the universe, she sought to recreate in her poetry. So many of her poems are acts of imaginative sympathy, when she has turned outwards from herself to see and appreciate the lives of others: the parents who care for a Down's syndrome child; the teenagers who question her at a poetry reading. This, in turn, leads to a sense of thanksgiving and praise. 'Gratitude' is a word and theme that often occurs: 'I want a music of pure thankfulness.' Her 1998 collection is entitled simply *Praises*. She has poems about nature in all its aspects, the changing seasons – especially spring – and others on a whole range of animals, including ants and rooks. Like Rupert Brooke in his poem 'The great love', with its theme 'These I love', Jennings has her own quirky list in *Praises*, beginning:

I praise those things I always take for granted –
The tap my sister turns on for my bath
Every time I stay, – the safety pin –
And who invented it? I do not know –
The comb, the piece of soap, a shoe, its shine . . .
I praise the yawning kind of sleep that's coming,
And where the spirit goes, the sheet, the pillow . . .

She has another poem on friendship with a lovely, gentle, lyrical quality that is as moving as the one I have chosen here. The one above, however, I love for her theme of 'gracious moments shining still', her 'list of love', which she finds 'full', and the way she counts her 'good hours'.[6]

Tuesday
The quality of sprawl

Les Murray

Sprawl is the quality
of the man who cut down his Rolls-Royce
into a farm utility truck, and sprawl
is what the company lacked when it made repeated
efforts
to buy the vehicle back and repair its image.
Sprawl is doing your farming by aeroplane, roughly,
or driving a hitchhiker that extra hundred miles home.
It is the rococo of being your own still centre.
It is never lighting cigars with ten-dollar notes:
that's idiot ostentation and murder of starving people.
Nor can it be bought with the ash of million-dollar deeds.
Sprawl lengthens the legs; it trains greyhounds on liver and
beer.
Sprawl almost never says Why not? With palms comically
raised
nor can it be dressed for, not even in running shoes worn
with mink and a nose ring. That is Society. That's Style.
Sprawl is more like the thirteenth banana in a dozen
or anyway the fourteenth.
Sprawl is Hank Stamper in *Never Give an Inch*
bisecting an obstructive official's desk with a chainsaw.
Not harming the official. Sprawl is never brutal
though it's often intransigent. Sprawl is never Simon de
Montfort

at a town-storming: Kill them all! God will know his own.
Knowing the man's name this was said to might be sprawl.
Sprawl occurs in art. The fifteenth to twenty-first
lines in a sonnet, for example. And in certain paintings;
I have sprawl enough to have forgotten which paintings.
Turner's glorious 'Burning of the Houses of Parliament'
comes to mind, a doubling bannered triumph of sprawl –
except, he didn't fire them.
Sprawl gets up the nose of many kinds of people
(every kind that comes in kinds) whose futures don't
          include it.
Some decry it as criminal presumption, silken-robed Pope
          Alexander
dividing the new world between Spain and Portugal.
If he smiled *in petto* afterwards, perhaps the thing did have
          sprawl.
Sprawl is really classless, though. It's John Christopher
          Frederick Murray
asleep in his neighbours' best bed in spurs and oilskins
but not having thrown up:
sprawl is never Calum who, drunk, along the hallways of
          our House,
reinvented the Festoon. Rather
it's Beatrice Miles going twelve hundred ditto in a taxi,

on the proceeds of her two-bob-a-sonnet Shakespeare
          readings.
An image of my country. And would that it were more so.
No, sprawl is full-gloss murals on a council-house wall.
Sprawl leans on things. It is loose-limbed in its mind.
Reprimanded and dismissed
it listens with a grin and one boot up on the rail
of possibility. It may have to leave the Earth.

Being roughly Christian, it scratches the other cheek
and thinks it unlikely. Though people have been shot for
    sprawl.

Les Murray (1938–2019)

Les Murray was brought up on a farm in Australia in some poverty. His mother died when he was 13, and his father collapsed. Murray said that he did not have any teenage years as he was looking after his father. From the age of 18, he wanted to be a poet and, before he died, he had had some 30 books of poetry published and had been translated into 11 languages. Regarded as the foremost Australian poet of his time, he won many awards. He celebrates many qualities of Australian life, as he does in 'Sprawl', which is, as he put it, 'an image of my country. And would that it were more so.'

When Murray got married, he became a Roman Catholic. His faith, though mostly hidden, is expressed in the celebration of all life, and is a fundamental feature of his poetry. In one poem, he proclaims, 'Religions are poems' and goes on to explore the ways in which this is true, culminating in the statement that:

God is . . . in the world as poetry
is in the poem, a law against its closure.

I fell in love with 'Sprawl' the first time I read it many years ago, and it still makes me smile and rejoice. If you would like a New Testament text for it, this would be St Paul's words, 'Be not conformed to this world' (Romans 12.2, KJV), for many of the vivid images are about rejecting what the world counts valuable, smart or fashionable. People buy a Rolls-Royce not just because it is a beautiful piece of engineering but also because it is a sign one has arrived. It will impress people, tell them one is wealthy or important or both. So the poem begins with the picture of a Rolls-Royce cut down to make a utility truck.

Although sprawl is an extreme form of not bothering too much about material things, it is not deliberate showing off. Lighting cigars with ten-dollar notes is deliberate ostentation and a waste of money that could help the poor. So the poem goes on in a series of arresting and unusual images. It can be shown in art when someone does not stick to the rules, and in a sonnet when it should have 14 lines but it has more. There is nothing stereotypical about this quality, for it can be shown in the most unusual ways. Nothing could seem less like it than the Pope dividing the world between Spain and Portugal, but suppose the Pope smiled in secret, knowing that it was an absurd gesture?

Although sprawl is a relaxed, carefree attitude to life that *in extremis* can get up the noses of the self-important, there is nothing deliberately hurtful about it. It goes out of its way to give a long lift to a hitchhiker. It is not brutal: 'No Lewd Advances. No Hitting Animals. No Speeding.' And although someone who sprawls might take liberties when they have had too much to drink, they would not actually be sick in someone else's house.

All this culminates with the wonderful image in the last verse, of the poet leaning against a fence with one foot up on the rail, an outward sign of an inner attitude. But then there is a final disturbing note: 'People have been shot for sprawl.' Individuals take themselves so seriously and so want to impress, that any refusal to take them seriously, any non-conformity, any cheek, is threatening. After all, Christ was crucified.

What is the secret of this successful way of life? The answer was given earlier. It is the 'rococo of being your own still centre'. Rococo was an architectural style that emerged in the early eighteenth century, developing on the earlier baroque style in a more playful, ornamental way. It comes from being at home in one's own skin, from a sense of one's own worth simply as oneself. And that, for a Christian, is rooted in the conviction that this is how we are for God.

Wednesday
If thou must love me . . .
(Sonnet 14)

Elizabeth Barrett Browning

If thou must love me, let it be for nought
Except for love's sake only. Do not say,
'I love her for her smile – her look – her way
Of speaking gently, – for a trick of thought
That falls in well with mine, and certes brought
A sense of pleasant ease on such a day' –
For these things in themselves, Belovèd, may
Be changed, or change for thee – and love, so wrought,
May be unwrought so. Neither love me for
Thine own dear pity's wiping my cheeks dry:
A creature might forget to weep, who bore
Thy comfort long, and lose thy love thereby!
But love me for love's sake, that evermore
Thou mayst love on, through love's eternity.

Elizabeth Barrett Browning (1806–1861)

Elizabeth Barrett Browning came from a wealthy family and was educated at home. A child prodigy, she started writing poems from the age of four and, at ten, was translating and writing in Greek. She read widely in all the printed classics of the day, in a variety of languages, including, later in life, the Hebrew Bible. From her teenage years, however, she suffered a serious, painful illness, for which she had to take laudanum and, later, morphine for the rest of her life.

Her poetry was hugely admired, including by Robert Browning, who wrote to tell her so. This led to one of the most famous courtships in the ninteenth century, conducted in secret because of the disapproval of her father. The couple married in secret, were disinherited by her father and lived most of the rest of their lives in Florence. Their relationship resulted in some of her most famous poems on love, including the one above.

Elizabeth Barrett Browning drew much admiration in her time, both in the UK and in the USA, and was an influence on Emily Dickinson. On the death of Wordsworth, she was a serious rival to Tennyson for the poet laureateship.

Although the Barrett family had made its fortune from slave plantations in the West Indies, Elizabeth was a strong abolitionist, as well as a campaigner against child labour. She was an admirer of Mary Wolstonecraft, and her reputation was revived by feminists in the twentieth century. She was passionately religious and wrote, 'Christ's religion is essentially poetry – poetry glorified.' She explored the religious aspect in many of her poems, especially in her early work, such as the sonnets.

At the beginning of any love relationship, people are attracted by particular features of the other person – a smile or sense of humour, the colour of the eyes or the shape of the body – but as love develops, the person is loved just for him- or herself. We can see this if we start to give reasons for why we might love someone. All the reasons in the end do not get to the heart of the matter. In fact, we might say that the best reason for love is that there is no reason. 'I love you because you are you,' someone might say. There is no higher reason than that.

In the poem above, Elizabeth Barrett Browning brings this out with great force. Everything about a person might change and, with age, we inevitably alter, becoming physically frail and sometimes mentally senile, so she says:

> But love me for love's sake, that evermore
> Thou mayst love on, through love's eternity.

Such love is a miracle and there is none greater, for it implies transcending the selfish, grasping ego to see and value the other for who he or she is. This reflects the way God sees us, and in that reflection there is supreme grace.

Thursday
The moor

R. S. Thomas

It was like a church to me.
I entered it on soft foot,
Breath held like a cap in the hand.
It was quiet.
What God was there made himself felt,
Not listened to, in clean colours
That brought a moistening of the eye,
In movement of the wind over grass.

There were no prayers said. But stillness
Of the heart's passions – that was praise
Enough; and the mind's cession
Of its kingdom. I walked on,
Simple and poor, while the air crumbled
And broke on me generously as bread.

R. S. Thomas (1913–2000)

R. S. Thomas read Latin at Bangor University and, after training at
St Michael's College, Llandaff, was ordained in the Church in Wales.
He served in a number of increasingly remote parishes, ending up at
Aberdaron on the Llŷn Peninsula and, finally, retiring to Y Rhiw, on
its south-west tip in 1978.

His first three volumes of verse were largely included in *Song at the
Year's Turning*, published in 1955 to great critical acclaim. He con-
tinued to publish slim volumes of verse throughout his ministry as a

parish priest. He was awarded the Queen's Gold Medal for poetry in 1964 and was nominated for the Nobel Prize in Literature in 1996. Brought up in an English-speaking family in Liverpool, he taught himself Welsh at the age of 30. He regretted that Welsh was not deeply enough part of him that he could write poetry in it, but he preferred to converse in Welsh and wrote some prose in the language, including an autobiography of himself in the third person. He was a fierce Welsh nationalist, and he wrote bitterly about the loss of the Welsh language and culture, castigating both the English for their takeover and the Welsh for their subservience to this.

When R. S. Thomas's *Song at the Year's Turning* was first published, it had an introduction by John Betjeman containing the words, 'The "Name" which has the honour to introduce this fine poet to a wider public will be forgotten long before that of R. S. Thomas.'[7] After the deaths of W. H. Auden and T. S. Eliot, he was the major English-language poet writing on religious themes in a way that resonated with unbelievers and believers alike. For the last part of the twentieth century, his poetry spoke more clearly than any other for and to the condition of all who raise the question of God in any serious way.

His early poems were mainly about the hard life of Welsh hill farmers, at a time when they still ploughed with horses. These poems often appear in school textbooks. His poetry went through a number of phases, some of them very uncompromising and shocking in their exploration of God. One of his themes is the apparent absence of God.

The fact that this absence is not an ordinary kind of absence reveals itself by the way it does not let us go, but haunts us. Thomas wrote both an essay in Welsh and a poem in English called 'Abercaug' on this theme. Literally, this means the place where the cuckoos sing, but it is a place we can never find. Wherever we look, it is not there; but this is not cause for despair. In the poem, he wrote:

An absence is how we become surer
of what we want. Abercaug
is not here now, but there. And
there is the indefinable point . . .

While Thomas wrote some of the bleakest poems in the English lan-
guage, he also wrote two of the most tender about his first wife when,
after a lifetime together, she died. In another poem called 'Arrival',
he wrote about being taken by surprise by an overwhelming truth
that 'There is everything to look forward to.'

The poem quoted above requires little comment. It is easy to see
him, with his gaunt, ascetic face, striding in the open country, hum-
ble and receptive to the natural world around him. This quietens his
perpetually questioning mind and, like one of the poor in spirit in
the Beatitudes, he receives the bread of life.[8]

Friday
The kingdom of God

Francis Thompson

'In no strange land'

O world invisible, we view thee,
O world intangible, we touch thee,
O world unknowable, we know thee,
Inapprehensible, we clutch thee!

Does the fish soar to find the ocean,
The eagle plunge to find the air –
That we ask of the stars in motion
If they have rumour of thee there?

Not where the wheeling systems darken,
And our benumbed conceiving soars! –
The drift of pinions, would we hearken,
Beats at our own clay-shuttered doors.

The angels keep their ancient places; –
Turn but a stone, and start a wing!
'Tis ye, 'tis your estranged faces,
That miss the many-splendoured thing.

But (when so sad thou canst not sadder)
Cry; – and upon thy so sore loss

Shall shine the traffic of Jacob's ladder
Pitched betwixt Heaven and Charing Cross.

Yea, in the night, my Soul, my daughter,
Cry, – clinging Heaven by the hems;
And lo, Christ walking on the water
Not of Gennesareth, but Thames!

Francis Thompson (1859–1907)

Francis Thompson's father was a doctor in Preston who had converted to Roman Catholicism. Francis was a shy but studious child at his Catholic school. Though not physically strong, he became an ardent, lifelong cricket fan. Urged by his father, Francis studied medicine at what is now the University of Manchester for six years, but he had no real interest in medicine and ran away to live in poverty in London, doing odd jobs, including selling matches. He took opium for his health and became addicted, living rough with other homeless people in the Charing Cross area. He contemplated suicide but was saved by a vision of Thomas Chatterton, the eighteenth-century poet who did kill himself at a young age. Eventually, he was given a home by a prostitute, whom he called his saviour.

In 1888, after three years on the streets, he sent some of his poems to the Meynells, a married couple who were publishers and who recognized their quality. In all, he published three volumes of poems, which were very well received. His most famous poem is 'The hound of heaven', in which God is thought of as pursuing us with 'deliberate speed, majestic instancy'. Thompson died in 1907 of tuberculosis.

In the wonderful poem above, the first verses depict our dwelling in the all-enveloping presence of God as fish live in the ocean, eagles in the air and stars in the sky. We don't have to look to space to find God; he 'beats at our own clay-shuttered doors' (perhaps Thompson is referring to the creation account in Genesis 2, when humanity is described as being made of clay). Heaven is all about us, 'The angels keep their ancient places;' it is only our estrangement that causes us to miss this many-splendoured thing. However, when all our human resources are exhausted and we turn to God in desperate need, we find Jacob's ladder, with angels ascending and descending, and see Christ walking on the Thames, not just in Charing Cross but wherever we may be.

Behind this verse is the famous story of Jacob's dream, in which he saw a ladder between heaven and earth, with angels going up and down it. When he woke up, he said that God was in that place (see Genesis 28.10–22). It is an image that is taken up in John 1.51, where Nathaniel, an Israelite without guile, is told he will see angels of God ascending and descending on the Son of Man, Jesus himself. He is the one in whom we see the glory of God. He is the one in whom heaven and earth, God and humanity are joined, never to be unjoined. We discover him in our need. Our needs are angels, as a friend once said to me. They open us to God and allow him through.

> But (when so sad thou canst not sadder)
> Cry; – and upon thy so sore loss
> Shall shine the traffic of Jacob's ladder
> Pitched betwixt Heaven and . . .

wherever we are.

Saturday
Prayer

Carol Ann Duffy

Some days, although we cannot pray, a prayer
utters itself. So, a woman will lift
her head from the sieve of her hands and stare
at the minims sung by a tree, a sudden gift.

Some nights, although we are faithless, the truth
enters our hearts, that small familiar pain;
then a man will stand stock-still, hearing his youth
in the distant Latin chanting of a train.

Pray for us now. Grade 1 piano scales
console the lodger looking out across
a Midlands town. Then dusk, and someone calls
a child's name as though they named their loss.

Darkness outside. Inside, the radio's prayer –
Rockall. Malin. Dogger. Finisterre.

Carol Ann Duffy (born 1955)

Carol Ann Duffy was born in the Gorbals, a poor part of Glasgow, to a family of Irish heritage. Her father's work took the family to Stafford, where she had a good education at Roman Catholic schools. She later went on to read Philosophy at the University of Liverpool.

At the age of 11, her teachers had recognized and encouraged her poetic talent. From its first publication, her poetry was appreciated and she has been awarded many prestigious prizes. Hers is poetry that is both highly popular and esteemed by literary critics. She is also a playwright. She was Poet Laureate from 2009 to 2019 and is currently Professor of Contemporary Poetry at Manchester Metropolitan University.

Of her own writing, Duffy has said, 'I'm not interested, as a poet, in words like "plash" – Seamus Heaney words, interesting words. I like to use simple words, but in a complicated way.' She told *The Observer*, 'Like the sand and the oyster, it's a creative irritant. In each poem, I'm trying to reveal a truth, so it can't have a fictional beginning.'[9]

Duffy has spoken of the influence of her religious upbringing on her poetry and also said in the same *Observer* article that 'poetry and prayer are very similar'. That influence is very clear in 'Prayer'. It is a poem that is full of sounds, the half-note of wind in the leaves of a tree, the sound of a train, the sound of someone practising the piano, the sound of a child's name being called in the dusk, the sound of the late-night shipping forecast. They are sounds heard by those on their own, lying awake at night; by the lonely lodger looking out of the window; by us, as we sit by the radio. These are mysterious, far-off, haunting sounds. Like the effect of birds in the poetry of Edward Thomas, or the sound of children's laughter hidden in the leaves of a tree in T. S. Eliot's *Four quartets*, they have an elusive quality that seems to call us elsewhere. It reminds us of our youth and our loss. They are far away, like the remote places in the forecast; not exactly comforting, for they can bring a pain, yet also in some way reassuring. All these sounds are themselves a kind of prayer, lifting our hearts beyond ourselves; a sudden gift, calling us, reminding us of something.

WEEK 3
GLORY IN THE
ORDINARY

Monday
Miracles

Walt Whitman

Why, who makes much of a miracle?
As to me I know of nothing else but miracles,
Whether I walk the streets of Manhattan,
Or dart my sight over the roofs of houses toward the sky,
Or wade with naked feet along the beach just in the edge of
      the water,
Or stand under trees in the woods,
Or talk by day with any one I love, or sleep in the bed at
      night with any one I love,
Or sit at table at dinner with the rest,
Or look at strangers opposite me riding in the car,
Or watch honey-bees busy around the hive of a summer
      forenoon,
Or animals feeding in the fields,
Or birds, or the wonderfulness of insects in the air,
Or the wonderfulness of the sundown, or of stars shining
      so quiet and bright,
Or the exquisite delicate thin curve of the new moon in
      spring;
These with the rest, one and all, are to me miracles,
The whole referring, yet each distinct and in its place.
To me every hour of the light and dark is a miracle,
Every cubic inch of space is a miracle,
Every square yard of the surface of the earth is spread with
      the same,

Every foot of the interior swarms with the same.
    To me the sea is a continual miracle,
    The fishes that swim – the rocks – the motion of the
        waves – the ships with men in them,
    What stranger miracles are there?

Walt Whitman (1819–1892)

Walt Whitman left school at the age of 11 and, throughout his life, had a succession of low-paid jobs as a printer, teacher, reporter and editor. During the American Civil War, he worked as a voluntary nurse with the wounded. He published his first book of poems, *Leaves of Grass*, at his own expense when he was 35. 'Miracles', under a slightly different title, was one of the poems included in it. He lost his job as a result of the book's publication, but it was well received by discriminating critics, and he has been an influence on American poetry ever since.

Writing in free verse with biblical cadences, praising nature, democracy, love and friendship in his persona as a rough working man, Whitman is regarded as the quintessential American poet. His sexuality, which was expressed in his poetry, was controversial at the time, as are his racial views now. He was well received in the UK. He was open to all religions but an adherent of none, believing God was both transcendent and immanent, and the soul was immortal, in a state of progressive development.

Traditionally, miracles have been thought of as events that do not follow the ordinary laws of nature but are brought about directly by God. Whitman deliberately subverts that view. For him, everything in life is sheer miracle, and he follows this through both in relation to the city and the country, and people and nature.

Tuesday
And that is your glory

Yehuda Amichai

I've yoked together my large silence and my small outcry
like an ox and an ass. I've been through low and through
   high.
I've been in Jerusalem, in Rome. And perhaps in Mecca
   anon.
But now God is hiding, and man cries Where have you gone.
And that is your glory.

Underneath the world, God lies stretched on his back,
always repairing, always things get out of whack.
I wanted to see him all, but I see no more
than the soles of his shoes and I'm sadder than I was before.
And that is his glory.

Even the trees went out once to choose a king.
A thousand times I've given my life one more fling.
At the end of the street somebody stands and picks:
this one and this one and this one and this one and this.
And that is your glory.

Perhaps like an ancient statue that has no arms
our life, without deeds and heroes, has greater charms.
Ungird my T-shirt, love; this was my final bout.
I fought all the knights, until the electricity gave out.
And that is my glory.

Rest your mind, it ran with me all the way,
it's exhausted now and needs to knock off for the day.
I see you standing by the wide-open fridge door, revealed
from head to toe in a light from another world.
And that is my glory.
and that is his glory.
and that is your glory.

Yehuda Amichai (1924–2000)

Yehuda Amichai was born in Germany but, in 1935, aged 12, he emigrated to Palestine. He fought as a volunteer for the British Army and, on his discharge, trained as a teacher, changing his name from Ludwig Pfeuffer to Yehuda Amichai, meaning 'my people lives'. He fought for Israel in the wars of the following decades, while teaching and writing – novels and stories as well as poetry. He won many prizes and was nominated for the Nobel Prize on many occasions.

Amichai's poetry is both accessible and highly respected by international critics. It reflects both individual experience and wider philosophical questions on the meaning of life and politics, and has an endearing quality. Brought up in a strictly Orthodox family, he wrote poetry, as in the one quoted above, that wrestles with the question of God. He said that the language of prayer is entirely natural to him. His poetry, written in Hebrew, contains many nuances that, according to critics, cannot really be captured in translation. Nevertheless, he has been translated into 40 languages.

In the first verse of the poem above, the poet laments the apparent absence of God, despite searching in his own experience and the world's religions. The paradox is that he proclaims this as God's glory.

The second verse brilliantly combines the image of God as a mechanic lying on his back under a car and the Jewish mystical idea of God repairing the world. This, in turn, is linked with the image of Moses, who could not see the glory of God, only his back. Again, this is said to be the Divine Glory. The third verse refers to Judges 9.8–15, in which an allegory is told about the trees choosing a king. The fourth verse compares the poet who has given his all, and is stripped down like a statue without arms. But, again, there is the paradox: 'And that is my glory.'

Finally, we have the wonderful closing verse when, exhausted, having given up, he sees someone standing by an open fridge door, revealed 'from head to toe in light from another world', and that is a three-fold glory – not only that of the poet but also that of the person seen and God. It's as though only when we have exhausted all the usual routes to see God and just relax, we see God all around us.

Wednesday
The glory

Edward Thomas

The glory of the beauty of the morning, –
The cuckoo crying over the untouched dew;
The blackbird that has found it, and the dove
That tempts me on to something sweeter than love;
White clouds ranged even and fair as new-mown hay;
The heat, the stir, the sublime vacancy
Of sky and meadow and forest and my own heart: –
The glory invites me, yet it leaves me scorning
All I can ever do, all I can be,
Beside the lovely of motion, shape, and hue,
The happiness I fancy fit to dwell
In beauty's presence. Shall I now this day
Begin to seek as far as heaven, as hell,
Wisdom or strength to match this beauty, start
And tread the pale dust pitted with small dark drops,
In hope to find whatever it is I seek,
Hearkening to short-lived happy-seeming things
That we know naught of, in the hazel copse?
Or must I be content with discontent
As larks and swallows are perhaps with wings?
And shall I ask at the day's end once more
What beauty is, and what I can have meant
By happiness? And shall I let all go,
Glad, weary, or both? Or shall I perhaps know
That I was happy oft and oft before,

Awhile forgetting how I am fast pent,
How dreary-swift, with naught to travel to,
Is Time? I cannot bite the day to the core.

Edward Thomas (1878–1917)

For most of his adult life, Edward Thomas earned a living as a writer of articles and books. He loved walking long distances in the English countryside and writing about what he saw and experienced. However, he had to keep churning out articles and books in order to keep his family solvent, and they were always short of money. He suffered from depression and this was one of the factors that led to the deterioration of his initially happy marriage.

It was only in 1914, at the prompting of the American poet Robert Frost, that Thomas started writing poetry. Although under no obligation to, because of his age, Thomas volunteered for the army, was sent to France and was killed in 1917. It is for the wonderful poems written during this short period of time that he is known today. Some – 'As the team's head brass', for example – describe the effect of the war at home, but most of them are about aspects of nature and the countryside. They have a haunting, elusive quality about them, as though he is being touched by something just out of reach. Although Thomas had no formal religion, like many others he was conscious of the tantalizing quality of beauty, which often touched him through the songs of birds.[10]

Glory is one of the key words in the Bible, especially in John's Gospel. It points to that sublime conjunction of beauty with truth and goodness that exists in God. For a Christian, this glory shines in the face of Jesus Christ, as Peter, James and John experienced when they saw him transfigured before them on the mountain. We too are to be transfigured, 'from glory to glory' (2 Corinthians 3.18, NKJV). For all of us, whether or not we share that faith, there are experiences of glory in nature, as Thomas captures so brilliantly in this poem.[11]

The poem begins with an experience that is, for many, one of the most beautiful of all, an early morning in summer. The glory in this scene tempts him 'to something sweeter than love'. It invites him but also makes him conscious of his own shortcomings before absolute beauty. He knows he is seeking something, that he is restless and discontent and still has questions about the nature of beauty and happiness. 'I cannot bite the day to the core.' It is a vivid image, suggesting the sweet beauty of that glorious day, which he wants to bite and take into himself, but, in the end, it remains outside his grasp. Beauty tantalizes him. It draws him, calls him, but he can't possess or consume it. This, for a Christian, is because it is meant to point to its fulfilment in our relationship with God, whom St Augustine addressed as 'Thou beauty most ancient and so fresh'.[12]

Thursday

Lines composed a few miles above Tintern Abbey, on revisiting the banks of the Wye during a tour, July 13, 1798

William Wordsworth

For nature then

(The coarser pleasures of my boyish days
And their glad animal movements all gone by)
To me was all in all. – I cannot paint
What then I was. The sounding cataract
Haunted me like a passion: the tall rock,
The mountain, and the deep and gloomy wood,
Their colours and their forms, were then to me
An appetite; a feeling and a love,
That had no need of a remoter charm,
By thought supplied, not any interest
Unborrowed from the eye. – That time is past,
And all its aching joys are now no more,
And all its dizzy raptures. Not for this
Faint I, nor mourn nor murmur; other gifts
Have followed; for such loss, I would believe,
Abundant recompense. For I have learned
To look on nature, not as in the hour
Of thoughtless youth; but hearing oftentimes
The still sad music of humanity,

Nor harsh nor grating, though of ample power
To chasten and subdue. – And I have felt
A presence that disturbs me with the joy
Of elevated thoughts; a sense sublime
Of something far more deeply interfused,
Whose dwelling is the light of setting suns,
And the round ocean and the living air,
And the blue sky, and in the mind of man:
A motion and a spirit, that impels
All thinking things, all objects of all thought,
And rolls through all things. Therefore am I still
A lover of the meadows and the woods
And mountains; and of all that we behold
From this green earth; of all the mighty world
Of eye, and ear, – both what they half create,
And what perceive; well pleased to recognise
In nature and the language of the sense
The anchor of my purest thoughts, the nurse,
The guide, the guardian of my heart, and soul
Of all my moral being.

William Wordsworth (1770–1850)

Wordsworth was born and brought up in the Lake District, and the feelings aroused then by its natural beauty deeply affected him and are reflected in much of his poetry. As a young man, he visited France during the early stages of the French Revolution and was much inspired by it. As he put it in *The Prelude*:

Bliss it was in that dawn to be alive
But to be young was very heaven.

After a period in Somerset and Dorset and a trip to Germany, he returned to the Lake District, where he lived with his wife Mary

Hutchinson and his sister Dorothy, the poet and diarist, to whom he was very close. Dove Cottage on Grasmere, where they lived, is the national shrine to Wordsworth. In 1795, he met Samuel Taylor Coleridge and, three years later, they published *Lyrical Ballads,* which changed the face of English poetry. In the preface to the second edition, Wordsworth defined poetry as 'the spontaneous overflow of powerful feelings' and said his new poetry would use 'the real language of men' and would avoid the 'poetic diction' common in the eighteenth century. His subjects were the poor, old and outcast, and children.

Wordsworth and Coleridge evolved a new kind of blank verse which was different from that of Shakespeare or Milton. Together they are regarded as the pioneers of the Romantic movement, with its emphases on the individual and personal feeling. Coleridge, as well as Robert Southey, lived near Wordsworth and together they are known as the Lake Poets. Wordsworth's views became more conservative as he grew old and he was a strong supporter of the Church of England. He obtained a position of great eminence in British life and became Poet Laureate.

In the poem above, Wordsworth remembers the carefree joy he experienced in the Lake District when he was young, bounding in the mountains like a roe, and contrasts that with his more serious feelings later. He then makes the classic statement of his understanding of God. People have sometimes thought of Wordsworth as a pantheist – one who thinks God and nature are all bound up together as one. He is better described as a pan*en*theist – that is, one who believes that God is in all things and can, therefore, be known in and through them. The orthodox Christian view is that God is both transcendent and immanent. Indeed, it is because he is transcendent that he can be immanent – in all things at the same time. Because he is in all things, we can be inspired, nurtured and sustained by God through them, as Wordsworth was through nature. This led him to a deep sense of gratitude. As he wrote in a letter to a friend:

Theologians may puzzle their heads about dogmas as they will, the religion of gratitude cannot mislead us. Of that we are sure, and gratitude is the handmaid to hope, and hope the harbinger of faith. I look abroad upon nature, I think of the best part of our species, I lean upon my friends, and I meditate upon the Scriptures, especially the Gospel of St John, and my creed rises up of itself, with the ease of an exhalation, yet a fabric of adamant.[13]

Friday
Jubilate Agno
Christopher Smart

For I will consider my Cat Jeoffry.

For he is the servant of the Living God duly and daily
    serving him.

For at the first glance of the glory of God in the East he
    worships in his way.

For is this done by wreathing his body seven times round
    with elegant quickness.

For then he leaps up to catch the musk, which is the bless-
    ing of God upon his prayer.

For he rolls upon prank to work it in.

For having done duty and received blessing he begins to
    consider himself.

For this he performs in ten degrees.

For first he looks upon his forepaws to see if they are clean.

For secondly he kicks up behind to clear away there.

For thirdly he works it upon stretch with the fore paws
    extended.

For fourthly he sharpens his paws by wood.

For fifthly he washes himself.

For sixthly he rolls upon wash.

For seventhly he fleas himself, that he may not be inter-
    rupted upon the beat.

For eighthly he rubs himself against a post.

For ninthly he looks up for his instructions.

For tenthly he goes in quest of food.

For having consider'd God and himself he will consider his
   neighbour.
For if he meets another cat he will kiss her in kindness.
For when he takes his prey he plays with it to give it [a]
   chance.
For one mouse in seven escapes by his dallying.
For when his day's work is done his business more properly
   begins.
For he keeps the Lord's watch in the night against the
   adversary.
For he counteracts the powers of darkness by his electrical
   skin and glaring eyes.
For he counteracts the Devil, who is death, by brisking
   about the life.
For in his morning orisons he loves the sun and the sun
   loves him.

Christopher Smart (1722–1771)

Christopher Smart, known as Kit to his friends, was one of the lead-
ing writers of the time and a close associate of figures such as Samuel
Johnson and Henry Fielding. He became engaged in a war of words
with other writers of the time, known as a 'paper war'. He got into
serious debt and, under circumstances that are still not clear, found
himself committed to a mental hospital, which in those days was
called a 'bedlam' or lunatic asylum. His only companion was his
cat Jeoffry. Like so many other human beings, not least during the
COVID pandemic, he found solace and consolation through a fellow
creature. In this long poem, some fifteen hundred lines, of which
this extract is only a fragment of a fragment, Smart observes and
describes the behaviour of Jeoffry with sheer delight.

   The role of animals in the divine purpose is a mysterious one.
What are they for? Poets such as D. H. Lawrence and Ted Hughes
have well captured the sense of mystery and otherness of the animal

world and left us pondering. Our best guess is what Kit Smart discovered: that they glorify God by being themselves. In the poem by Gerard Manley Hopkins that is considered on pages 105–7, everything in nature does one thing and the same:

goes itself; *myself* it speaks and spells,
Crying *Whát I dó is me: for that I came.*

No one, except perhaps T. S. Eliot in his poems on cats, has captured this truth better than Smart. His poem exults in all the physical movements of his cat, and rejoices in Jeoffry's every form of play. There are some wonderful lines, not included above, which beautifully convey that sense of playfulness: 'for he can spraggle and waggle at the word of command',

For he is a mixture of gravity and waggery.
For he knows that God is his Saviour.

Saturday
Ode on a Grecian urn

John Keats

Thou still unravish'd bride of quietness,
Thou foster-child of silence and slow time,
Sylvan historian, who canst thus express
A flowery tale more sweetly than our rhyme:
What leaf-fring'd legend haunts about thy shape
Of deities or mortals, or of both,
In Tempe or the dales of Arcady?
What men or gods are these? What maidens loth?
What mad pursuit? What struggle to escape?
What pipes and timbrels? What wild ecstasy?

Heard melodies are sweet, but those unheard
Are sweeter; therefore, ye soft pipes, play on;
Not to the sensual ear, but, more endear'd,
Pipe to the spirit ditties of no tone:
Fair youth, beneath the trees, thou canst not leave
Thy song, nor ever can those trees be bare;
Bold Lover, never, never canst thou kiss,
Though winning near the goal yet, do not grieve;
She cannot fade, though thou hast not thy bliss,
For ever wilt thou love, and she be fair!

Ah, happy, happy boughs! that cannot shed
Your leaves, nor ever bid the Spring adieu;
And, happy melodist, unwearied,

Forever piping songs forever new;
More happy love! more happy, happy love!
    Forever warm and still to be enjoy'd,
    Forever panting, and forever young;
All breathing human passion far above,
    That leaves a heart high-sorrowful and cloy'd,
    A burning forehead, and a parching tongue.

Who are these coming to the sacrifice?
    To what green altar, O mysterious priest,
Lead'st thou that heifer lowing at the skies,
    And all her silken flanks with garlands drest?
What little town by river or sea shore,
    Or mountain-built with peaceful citadel,
    Is emptied of this folk, this pious morn?
And, little town, thy streets for evermore
    Will silent be; and not a soul to tell
    Why thou art desolate, can e'er return.

O Attic shape! Fair attitude! with brede
    Of marble men and maidens overwrought,
With forest branches and the trodden weed;
    Thou, silent form, dost tease us out of thought
As doth eternity: Cold Pastoral!
    When old age shall this generation waste,
    Thou shalt remain, in midst of other woe
Than ours, a friend to man, to whom thou say'st,
    'Beauty is truth, truth beauty, – that is all
    Ye know on earth, and all ye need to know.'

John Keats (1795–1821)

The father of John Keats looked after horses at the Swan and Hoop
Inn, which he later managed, not far from where Moorgate Station

is today. He died when Keats was 8 years old, so the boy was brought up mainly by his grandmother; his mother died when he was 14. He received a good education at a small private school and was apprenticed to a surgeon and apothecary before going on to train for medicine at Guy's Hospital, now part of King's College, London. However, the desire to write poetry continually battled with his medical training and he eventually gave it up to write full time, moving to Hampstead, to what is now Keat's Grove. He had great money difficulties and became increasingly ill with tuberculosis. He moved to Rome for his health, but died there at the age of 25.

Keats wrote poems for only six years, and published for only four. They received mainly hostile reviews but he had a few devoted admirers who saw his genius, which came to be recognized increasingly in the decades that followed, so that today he is noted and loved as one of the major British poets. He belongs, with Byron, to the second wave of the Romantic poets, whose emphasis was on emotions roused by the senses.

All human beings are conscious of the mystery of time – the fact that we live with a past, a present and a future – and the even greater mystery of the relation of time to a possible eternity. St Augustine gave a significant part of his *Confessions* over to writing about this. Few have raised such questions so beautifully and briefly as Keats did in this ode.

The poem above begins with the poet looking at a Greek vase that has on it a familiar scene of nature and the gods. He is brought up short by its sheer stillness. It is an 'unravish'd bride of quietness' and 'foster-child of silence and slow time'. It is highly likely that T. S. Eliot had this poem in mind when, in 'Burnt Norton', he refers to the stillness of a Chinese jar as that which words and music reach after.

Keats suggests that the artist who painted the vase succeeded in depicting the scene in a way that his poetry cannot. Then, instead of just looking at the scene, he imagines himself actually there, in the past. The unheard music of this imaginative engagement is even sweeter than memories of heard music, for we can catch the scene in a way that never fades or dies. It exists in the now for ever. This leaves us longing for a similar state where nothing decays and dies.

Then, in the third verse, Keats imagines not just the lover and the pipes but also the sacrifice the whole village is turning up to see, and he wonders where this is and what is going on. Finally, he notes that this silent scene 'dost tease us out of thought, as doth eternity'. Its unchanging movement in stillness without change raises the question, how are we to imagine eternity? Then come the often quoted lines, suggesting that what this beautiful work of art really says to us is:

Beauty is truth, truth beauty, – that is all
Ye know on earth, and all ye need to know.

A Christian will both want to learn from that statement and qualify it. For the first fifteen hundred years of the Church's existence, beauty as much as goodness and truth were all seen as fundamental to our understanding of God. Since the Reformation, sadly, the concept of beauty has been downplayed and is regarded by most people as the preserve of the arts, though now it is often banished from there as well. But as the great theologian Hans Urs von Balthasar wrote, whoever sneers at the concept of beauty as though it belonged to the past, whether they admit it or not, 'can no longer pray and soon will no longer be able to love'.[14] Equally, a Christian will want to say that we need to know more than Keats allows. For in beauty, properly understood, there is an integral relationship with both truth and goodness, and this finds its focus in the glory of God revealed in Jesus:

For it is the God who said, 'Let light shine out of darkness', who has shone in our hearts to give the light of the knowledge of the glory of God in the face of Jesus Christ.
(2 Corinthians 4.6, NRSV)

WEEK 4
PARENTAL LOVE

Monday
Oh antic God

Lucille Clifton

oh antic God
return to me
my mother in her thirties
leaned across the front porch
the huge pillow of her breasts
pressing against the rail
summoning me in for bed.

I am almost the dead woman's age times two.

I can barely recall her song
the scent of her hands
though her wild hair scratches my dreams
at night. return to me, oh Lord of then
and now, my mother's calling,
her young voice humming my name.

Lucille Clifton (1936–2010)

Lucille Clifton was brought up in Buffalo, New York, and attended
Howard University. Her family were enslaved from Dahomey, now
Benin, and her mother taught her to be proud of being a Dahomey
woman. She married a professor of philosophy and sculpture and
they had six children. Her first book of poetry was published in 1969
and was well received. During the course of her career, Clifton held
a number of prestigious academic posts and received many prizes

for her poetry. Her book *Two-headed Woman* won the 1980 Juniper Prize. It contained her poem 'Homage to my hips', which marked the beginning of her interest in 'the transgressive black body'.[15] In the poem above and 'Homage to my hair', she challenged stereotypes and celebrated the African American body as a source of power, sexuality, pride and freedom. She was also a much respected writer of books for children.

In the poem above, we are immediately struck by the word 'antic'. We speak of people being 'up to their antics', up to their tricks – hopefully in a playful manner. So what trick is God up to? What is he playing at?

The poet has a vivid memory, a mental postcard from her childhood, of her warm, physical mother calling her to bed. The image brings with it a great sense of longing to have that physical presence again. Then, in a one-line shock, Clifton realizes that she is almost twice the age her mother was then. She notes how memories fade but this makes her long even more. But what is she longing for at this stage? It seems it is God she wants to return; the God she associates with her childhood: 'return to me, oh Lord of then'. With that returning God, though, she wants to hear again the young voice of her mother not just calling, but calling with such warmth and welcome and happiness that it is a kind of humming.

Tuesday
The almond tree

Jon Stallworthy

1
All the way to the hospital
the lights were green as peppermints.
Trees of black iron broke into leaf
ahead of me, as if
I were the lucky prince
in an enchanted wood
summoning summer with my whistle,
banishing winter with a nod.

Swung by the road from bend to bend,
I was aware that blood was running
down through the delta of my wrist
and under arches
of bright bone. Centuries,
continents it had crossed;
from an undisclosed beginning
spiralling to an unmapped end.

2
Crossing (at sixty) Magdalen Bridge
Let it be a son, a son, said
the man in the driving mirror,
Let it be a son. The tower

held up its hand: the college
bells shook their blessing on his head.

3
I parked in an almond's
shadow blossom, for the tree
was waving, waving me
upstairs with a child's hands.

4
Up
the spinal stair
and at the top
along
a bone-white corridor
the blood tide swung
me swung me to a room
whose walls shuddered
with the shuddering womb.
Under the sheet
wave after wave, wave
after wave beat
on the bone coast, bringing
ashore – whom?
        New –
minted, my bright farthing!
Coined by our love, stamped with
our images, how you
enrich us! Both
you make one. Welcome
to your white sheet,
my best poem!

5

At seven-thirty
the visitors' bell
scissored the calm
of the corridors.
The doctor walked with me
to the slicing doors.
His hand upon my arm,
his voice – *I have to tell
you* – set another bell
beating in my head:
your son is a mongol
the doctor said.

6

How easily the word went in –
clean as a bullet
leaving no mark on the skin,
stopping the heart within it.

This was my first death.
The 'I' ascending on a slow
last thermal breath
studied the man below

as a pilot treading air might
the buckled shell of his plane –
boot, glove and helmet
feeling no pain

from the snapped wires' radiant ends.
Looking down from a thousand feet

I held four walls in the lens
of an eye; wall, window, the street

a torrent of windscreens, my own
car under its almond tree,
and the almond waving me down.
I wrestled against gravity,

but light was melting and the gulf
cracked open. Unfamiliar
the body of my late self
I carried to the car.

7

The hospital – its heavy freight
lashed down ship-shape ward over ward –
steamed into the night with some on board
soon to be lost if the desperate

charts were known. Others would come
altered to land or find the land
altered. At their voyage's end
some would be added to, some

diminished. In a numbered cot
my son sailed from me; never to come
ashore into my kingdom
speaking my language. Better not

look that way. The almond tree
was beautiful in labour. Blood-
dark, quickening, bud after bud
split, flower after flower shook free.

On the darkening wind a pale
face floated. Out of reach. Only when
the buds, all the buds, were broken
would the tree be in full sail.

In labour the tree was becoming
itself. I, too, rooted in earth
and ringed by darkness, from the death
of myself saw myself blossoming,

wrenched from the caul of my thirty
years' growing, fathered by my son,
unkindly in a kind season
by love shattered and set free.

Jon Stallworthy (1935–2014)

Jon Stallworthy began writing poems when he was seven and won
the Newdigate Prize for poetry when he was at Oxford. He made
his reputation as a biographer of Wilfred Owen and as a special-
ist in First World War poetry, and later with a biography of Louis
MacNeice. He was Professor of English at Cornell University and
then at Oxford. As an accomplished poet, he published a number of
well-received volumes. One was inspired by the lives and letters of
his ancestors in New Zealand in the nineteenth century.

The first verses of the poem above describe the poet rushing to
hospital in excitement for the birth of his first child. Then, when he
learns the boy has Down's syndrome, we have the total change of
mood as he goes back to the almond tree where his car is parked.
First, the sense of being in a plane that has been shot down, and
then the thought of his son sailing to him but never able to come
ashore to a land that spoke his language. Finally, as he looks at the
branches of the almond tree, which had waved him cheerfully on
his way, he sees the buds breaking and knows he himself has been

given a harsh birth into a hard reality. Still, there is love and in that love he is free.

The poem moves wonderfully from the sense of excitement through total heartbreak to a hard but positive conclusion. You can almost see the father bounding up the stairs to the ward in the beginning, and trudging back across the car park, lost in desolation after receiving the news.

There are few people more heroic than parents who look after children who suffer some form of disorder or disability. There is the permanent limitation on the activities they are able to engage in, the constant care they are required to give, the endless visits to hospital. For those in such a position, their lives are totally changed from what they were before the birth, and from what they were expecting them to be like after. Amazingly, so many parents in such a position somehow find the inner resources to be able to cope. They show love in its most testing and unremitting form. Often, they are rewarded. It is well known that children suffering from Down's syndrome, for example, are often hugely affectionate. Those diagnosed with autism, which has a very wide spectrum of presenting symptoms, sometimes have intellectual capacities approaching genius. So these children are not so much impaired as differently abled.

Some conditions are so severe that it is impossible, even for the most loving parents, to cope with them at home and the children have to be looked after in specialist surroundings. It is a sign of a civilized country that it is willing to offer help to those parents who look after their children and provide specialist homes for children whose parents cannot look after them. All such children are children of God, uniquely valuable in themselves as themselves.

John Stallworthy brings out the utter heartbreak of a parent first learning that there is something not right about his newborn child, but he sees this experience also as a kind of hard second birth for himself into a testing adulthood of love.

Wednesday

Walking away

C. Day-Lewis

It is eighteen years ago, almost to the day –
A sunny day with leaves just turning,
The touch-lines new-ruled – since I watched you play
Your first game of football, then, like a satellite
Wrenched from its orbit, go drifting away
Behind a scatter of boys. I can see
You walking away from me towards the school
With the pathos of a half-fledged thing set free
Into a wilderness, the gait of one
Who finds no path where the path should be.
That hesitant figure, eddying away
Like a winged seed loosened from its parent stem,
Has something I never quite grasp to convey
About nature's give-and-take – the small, the scorching
Ordeals which fire one's irresolute clay.
I have had worse partings, but none that so
Gnaws at my mind still. Perhaps it is roughly
Saying what God alone could perfectly show –
How selfhood begins with a walking away,
And love is proved in the letting go.

C. Day-Lewis (1904–1972)

Day-Lewis, the son of a clergyman, was of Irish extraction. At Oxford, he was part of the circle round W. H. Auden and one of the voices of the generation that preceded the Second World War. His first volume of poems appeared when he was 21. During the war, he worked for the Ministry of Information and, afterwards, wrote detective stories under the name Nicholas Blake to earn an income, its not usually being possible to live on the money made from writing poetry alone. In 1960, he denounced the Communist Party, of which he had previously been a member. He was very much part of the literary establishment of his time, and was both Professor of Poetry at Oxford and Poet Laureate.

In the poem above, the poet brings to mind a vivid memory from eighteen years before. It is autumn, the beginning of the school year, and, as a loving parent, he is watching his son play his first game of football. After the game, the boy, instead of seeking out his father as he might have done earlier, goes off in a crowd of the other boys. He has his own life with them now. Although this is only a tiny incident, it is one of a number of scorching ordeals we experience as human beings. Life would bring many partings, but this one clearly gnawed at Day-Lewis's mind with its wider lesson.

Saying what God alone could perfectly show –
How selfhood begins with a walking away,
And love is proved in the letting go.

Those three lines are profoundly true and in them is contained a deep theological point: 'Love is proved in the letting go.' When God said, 'Let there be . . . ', he gave the universe a life of its own. It was given the freedom, within the essential constraints of what we call the laws of nature, to go its own way. Indeed, to be created is to have a life of one's own. That freedom becomes conscious and self-conscious in us human beings. We can, within certain limits, shape our own future. Then, when Christ comes among us, we are again left free to respond or not. We are not coerced.

God's amazing love is shown first of all in bringing independent life into existence, life that can turn its back on its creator and spurn its divine redeemer. As the poem says, God alone could perfectly show such letting go, but doing so is an essential prerequisite of our existence as selves. We can only be a self if we can make our own choices and fashion our own future. That is the gift we have been given.

Thursday
Mother to son

Langston Hughes

Well, son, I'll tell you:
Life for me ain't been no crystal stair.
It's had tacks in it,
And splinters,
And boards torn up,
And places with no carpet on the floor –
Bare.
But all the time
I'se been a-climbin' on,
And reachin' landin's,
And turnin' corners,
And sometimes goin' in the dark
Where there ain't been no light.
So boy, don't you turn back.
Don't you set down on the steps
'Cause you finds it's kinder hard.
Don't you fall now –
For I'se still goin', honey,
I'se still climbin',
And life for me ain't been no crystal stair.

Langston Hughes (1901–1967)

As his father left shortly after he was born, Langston Hughes was mainly brought up by his grandmother in the American Midwest. He was a prolific writer from an early age, and when he dropped out of Columbia University, he wrote poetry, did odd jobs and travelled.

His poems started appearing in *The Crisis*, the magazine of 'the National Association for the Advancement of Colored People (NAACP), and his first book of poems was published in 1926. He settled in Brooklyn and is, above all, associated with the Harlem Renaissance, in which poetry, jazz and theatre influenced one another. Hughes wrote novels and short stories as well as poetry and, during the early stirrings of the civil rights movement, wrote a weekly column for the *Chicago Defender*, the leading African American newspaper. He won many prizes and awards.

Both of his paternal great-grandmothers were enslaved Africans, and both of his paternal great-grandfathers were slave owners. The main theme of his poetry is the celebration of African American life and culture. In 1926, he wrote:

The younger Negro artists who create now intend to express our individual dark-skinned selves without fear or shame. If white people are pleased we are glad. If they are not, it doesn't matter. We know we are beautiful. And ugly, too. The tom-tom cries, and the tom-tom laughs. If colored people are pleased we are glad. If they are not, their displeasure doesn't matter either. We build our temples for tomorrow, strong as we know how, and we stand on top of the mountain free within ourselves.[16]

Hughes found the Black Power movement too angry, and some other African American writing too middle-class. He wanted to celebrate the joy, as well as recognizing the faults, of poorer people. His raising of racial self-consciousness as a matter of pride was an inspiration for artists, including those writers throwing off the legacy of European colonialism.

This affirmation of African American life, and the courage, resolution and pride it entailed, is very much the mood of the poem above, about a mother who, like so many African American mothers, had a hard life. There is no self-pity in it, just fortitude and determination, and the example she wants to pass on to her son:

Don't you fall now –
For I'se still goin', honey,
I'se still climbin',
And life for me ain't been no crystal stair.

Friday
Digging

Seamus Heaney

Between my finger and my thumb
The squat pen rests; snug as a gun.

Under my window, a clean rasping sound
When the spade sinks into gravelly ground:
My father, digging. I look down

Till his straining rump among the flowerbeds
Bends low, comes up twenty years away
Stooping in rhythm through potato drills
Where he was digging.

The coarse boot nestled on the lug, the shaft
Against the inside knee was levered firmly.
He rooted out tall tops, buried the bright edge deep
To scatter new potatoes that we picked,
Loving their cool hardness in our hands.

By God, the old man could handle a spade.
Just like his old man.

My grandfather cut more turf in a day
Than any other man on Toner's bog.
Once I carried him milk in a bottle
Corked sloppily with paper. He straightened up

To drink it, then fell to right away
Nicking and slicing neatly, heaving sods
Over his shoulder, going down and down
For the good turf. Digging.

The cold smell of potato mould, the squelch and slap
Of soggy peat, the curt cuts of an edge
Through living roots awaken in my head.
But I've no spade to follow men like them.

Between my finger and my thumb
The squat pen rests.
I'll dig with it.

Seamus Heaney (1939–2013)

Seamus Heaney was one of nine children born to a farming family in Bellaghy, in Northern Ireland, where he is buried. He always considered himself Irish. After Queen's College, Belfast, where his interest in poetry was aroused, he taught at St Joseph's, a teacher-training college. His book *Death of a Naturalist* was published in 1966 to wide critical acclaim. He held professorships in both the USA and Oxford, and won innumerable prizes and awards, including the Nobel Prize in Literature in 1995. A poet of towering stature, he was, in his time, the best-known poet in the world.

The strength of this poem is the combination of sound and sight that runs right through it. The poet is sitting at his desk writing and, first of all, it is a sound he hears – outside his window. It is the clean, rasping sound of a spade sinking into gravelly ground. The sound gives rise to an image of his father 20 years before, bending low, stooping in rhythm, digging determinedly: 'By God, the old man could handle a spade.' So too could his grandfather, digging peat out of a bog. A memory of himself as a young boy comes to mind, of taking some milk to his grandfather and his scarcely pausing before getting back to 'nicking and slicing neatly, heaving sods', all the time digging down and down. Then, in a wonderful combination, smell, sound and sight are brought together as the memory comes to the forefront of his mind with total clarity. The poem concludes and, though Heaney has no spade, the strength and skill he knew his father and grandfather to possess will find new expression in himself, as his pen digs deep using words.

Saturday
Taking a chance

Richard Harries

'Let there be life', he said, or was it she?
'atom, star, cell and plant – simply let them be'.
'No', D said, 'they will only clash and kill.'
'Yes', she replied, 'and combine with good will.
So let some know that their life is their own
And grow by reaping the seed they have sown.'
'Stop there' said D, 'They will hurt and destroy
All I foresee are seven walls of Troy.'
'I will imbue them with hope', she replied,
'my love will draw the world close to my side.
I will take the risk and enter their life,
expose my heart and let it bear their strife.
I will let him go there, to crib and grave
From out of their self-made hells he will save.
I will cradle the world as Mary the child
And Christ will hold their love, however wild.
I will take the chance without foreseeing
They can choose, or not, to give thanks for being.'

Richard Harries (born 1936)

By including one of my own poems in this book, I am not pre-
tending that it is of the same quality as the others. It is simply that
it says something about parental love I have not been able to find
elsewhere.

The poem reflects a dialogue in the Divine Mind. The letter 'D' does not mean anything in particular. It does not stand for the devil – the word 'doubt' comes closer to what is intended.

The background to the poem is provided by Ivan Karamazov's great challenge in Dostoevsky's novel *The Brothers Karamazov*. Ivan tells some horrific stories of cruelty to his children and then says, 'It is not that I don't believe in God, Alyosha, it's just that I return him the ticket.' This is the beginning of the modern protest against God that, for example, appears in Albert Camus. What Ivan's protest amounts to is that it would have been better for God not to have created the world in the first place. The implication of this is that it would have been better if we had not been born. The Divine Mind is heard facing this argument in the poem.

Humans will indeed clash and kill, hurt and destroy, but the Divine Life will enter human life and, from within the flux of events, save people from themselves. He does not foresee how things will turn out, but will experience human life from the inside and let people choose for themselves whether or not they are glad to have lived. He will take a chance. This is a choice we can make only for ourselves. We can never make it for anyone else.[17]

The poem is written in heroic couplets of ten syllables in each line, which are pairs of lines in iambic pentameter that rhyme – the form associated with the poets of the Augustan age: Pope and Dryden. There is a deliberate ambiguity about the gender of the Divine. The male stereotype at the beginning is questioned. The voice that is willing to be enclosed in crib and grave is feminine. The child who is born is masculine.

As I shaped this poem, I asked my daughter to draw a Christmas card to go with it. She depicted a young woman against a starry sky holding a babe in her arms. The babe was holding a globe. This is Mary and the Christ Child, but also the Divine Love creating the world and sending its redeemer. Taking a chance.

WEEK 5
BEING FULLY
HUMAN

Monday

As kingfishers catch fire, dragonflies draw flame

Gerard Manley Hopkins

As kingfishers catch fire, dragonflies draw flame;
As tumbled over rim in roundy wells
Stones ring; like each tucked string tells, each hung bell's
Bow swung finds tongue to fling out broad its name;
Each mortal thing does one thing and the same:
Deals out that being indoors each one dwells;
Selves – goes itself; *myself* it speaks and spells,
Crying *Whát I dó is me: for that I came.*

I say móre: the just man justices;
Keeps grace: thát keeps all his goings graces;
Acts in God's eye what in God's eye he is –
Chríst – for Christ plays in ten thousand places,
Lovely in limbs, and lovely in eyes not his
To the Father through the features of men's faces.

Gerard Manley Hopkins (1844–1889)

Gerard Manley Hopkins was influenced by the Oxford Movement and became a devout Anglo-Catholic. Then, like others such as John Henry Newman, he became a member of the Roman Catholic Church and then a Jesuit priest. He destroyed all his earlier poetry but later started to write again in a unique, innovative style, though none was published until after his death. Since then, he has been recognized as one of the great poets of his and any age.

Some of Hopkins' poetry is wonderfully celebratory of life, especially nature, but in Dublin, where he spent his last years, it became very dark. The conditions he lived in were unhygienic and he suffered from poor health. He had to spend much of his time marking scripts and doing other tedious work that allowed no expression to his creativity. His last poems are almost outpourings of despair.[18]

The poem above, however, was written in a happier time. The first verse looks at what happens in nature. Everything, whether a kingfisher, dragonfly or stone, has a unique identity and its purpose is simply to be itself: '*Whát I dó is me: for that I came*'. Here, as elsewhere in his poetry, he was influenced by Duns Scotus, the thirteenth-century Scottish philosopher, for whom what mattered was the 'isness' of things, their sheer existence and unique individuality.

In the second verse, Hopkins looks at human beings and says that exactly the same principle applies to us. We are to be ourselves, but we are ourselves only when we act justly, when we allow God's grace to make everything we do graceful. When that happens, we are what we are meant to be. That is how we are in the eyes of God and is nothing less than Christ. St Paul wrote of 'the riches of the glory of this mystery, which is Christ in you, the hope of glory' (Colossians 1.27, NRSV). This Christ is not just incarnate in Jesus but also in all those who believe in his name, who are limbs or members of his body. So it is that, as Hopkins writes it:

Christ plays in ten thousand places,
Lovely in limbs, and lovely in eyes not his
To the Father through the features of men's faces.

Over the past 60 years or so, we have been told endless times to be ourselves, but what is that self we are meant to be? We are, most of us, such a mixture of conflicting emotions and drives. The Christian answer is quite clear: our true self, our soul's soul, is nothing less than Christ in us.

Tuesday
On imagination

Phyllis Wheatley

Thy various works, imperial queen, we see,
How bright their forms! how deck'd with pomp by thee!
Thy wond'rous acts in beauteous order stand,
And all attest how potent is thine hand.

From *Helicon's* refulgent heights attend,
Ye sacred choir, and my attempts befriend:
To tell her glories with a faithful tongue,
Ye blooming graces, triumph in my song.

Now here, now there, the roving *Fancy* flies,
Till some lov'd object strikes her wand'ring eyes,
Whose silken fetters all the senses bind,
And soft captivity involves the mind.
Imagination! who can sing thy force?

Or who describe the swiftness of thy course?
Soaring through air to find the bright abode,
Th' empyreal palace of the thund'ring God,
We on thy pinions can surpass the wind,
And leave the rolling universe behind:
From star to star the mental optics rove,
Measure the skies, and range the realms above.
There in one view we grasp the mighty whole,
Or with new worlds amaze th' unbounded soul.

Phyllis Wheatley (1753–1784)

Phyllis Wheatley was born in either Gambia or Senegal and, about the age of seven, she was sold into slavery by a local chief. The slave ship that took her to Boston was called *Phyllis* and that was the name she was given by the prosperous family who purchased her. She was given their surname, Wheatley, as was the custom at the time. Encouraged to read by the family, especially the children, by the age of 10, she was reading Latin and Greek classics in the original and, at the age of 12, wrote her first poems. She was given a special status in the family and was spared the chores done by other slaves.

In 1773, at the age of 20, Wheatley accompanied her master, Nathaniel Wheatley to London. This was partly for her health, for she suffered from chronic asthma, but really to get her poems published, which they were. She met various influential people, and a meeting was also arranged with George III, though it did not take place as she had returned to America by the chosen date. The publication of her poems brought her fame on both sides of the Atlantic and she was praised by, among others, George Washington.

Wheatley was released from slavery by her patrons, the Wheatley family, but they died shortly afterwards. She married a poor, similarly freed black man, John Peters, who ran a small business. Conditions for freed black people were particularly tough at the time and so the couple lived in poverty. Wheatley's three children died, as did she at the age of 31.

In all, Wheatley wrote about 145 poems and is honoured as the first published African American poet, and as one who earned her living by writing. Scholars in the 1960s were critical of her apparent acceptance of her slave status, but this view has changed. Further research has revealed her disdain for slavery as being contrary to God's justice. Her poetry, though drawing on classical and biblical allusions in the style of the time, nevertheless shows an originality in the ways in which they are used.

In the poem above, the imperial queen who is praised is the imagination. The imagination enables us to see the universe in a wondrous light. Helicon is the mountain in Greek mythology near the Gulf of Corinth, down which flow the two springs of the muses, whose help she seeks to extol imagination. As her mind roves over the world, she finds herself entranced. Imagination has endless power to transport her and, by using it, the soul is unfettered.

The poem has three more verses, in which winter sets in and binds her again, leaving her facing reality. Critics therefore see in this poem not just the power of the imagination to give us unbounded freedom, even when we are in captivity, but also the reality of a world in which such captivity – slavery in Wheatley's case – remains a harsh reality. For Coleridge, our human imagination is the source of all creativity and is a reflection of a primary creative imagination in God himself. As such, it is part of what it means to be made in the image of God. Even as a slave, therefore, Wheatley could use her imagination to range over the universe and praise its Creator.

Wednesday
An Essay on Man (Epistle II)
Alexander Pope

Know then thyself, presume not God to scan;
The proper study of mankind is man.
Plac'd on this isthmus of a middle state,
A being darkly wise, and rudely great:
With too much knowledge for the sceptic side,
With too much weakness for the stoic's pride,
He hangs between; in doubt to act, or rest;
In doubt to deem himself a god, or beast;
In doubt his mind or body to prefer;
Born but to die, and reas'ning but to err;
Alike in ignorance, his reason such,
Whether he thinks too little, or too much:
Chaos of thought and passion, all confus'd;
Still by himself abus'd, or disabus'd;
Created half to rise, and half to fall;
Great lord of all things, yet a prey to all;
Sole judge of truth, in endless error hurl'd:
The glory, jest, and riddle of the world!

Alexander Pope (1688–1744)

Alexander Pope had a difficult life. He suffered from tuberculosis of
the spine, which left him with a hunchback. He had to wear a corset
in order to stand straight and was permanently in pain. Relatively
short too, he was mocked by his contemporaries. He was a Roman
Catholic, which at that time meant he could not go to a good school

or university or hold public office. He also had to live ten miles outside London, eventually settling in Twickenham.

Pope was first taught by an aunt and then self-educated by reading books. He knew a range of languages, including Greek, and discovered Homer at the age of six. He found immediate fame with his first poems and is usually reckoned the finest poet of the Augustan age. At that time, the first half of the eighteenth century, Pope and other writers sought to emulate the high literary standards of Rome under Augustus Caesar, their work being characterized by wit and conceit, satire and classical allusion. Later in the eighteenth century, there was a reaction against the rigidity of their style by the artists of the Romantic age, who put an emphasis on feeling instead. In the twentieth century, the virtues of the Augustans were rediscovered.

Pope was a satirist and he bitterly lampooned the politicians and leading men of the age. Politically, he was a Whig, but his fellow satirist Jonathan Swift, the Tory Dean of St Patrick's, Dublin, was a friend despite political differences. Although he was primarily a satirist, Pope also saw himself as a moralist, which is reflected in his *An Essay on Man*. As we have it at the moment, this consists of two epistles totalling 18 sections and 40 verses, written to his friend Lord Bolingbroke. He planned that this would be part of a longer work, but Pope died before it was completed. Like Milton's epic poem, *Paradise Lost*, Pope saw the main purpose of his poem as being to justify the ways of God to humanity. It is written in his favourite verse form, heroic couplets, which are pairs of rhyming lines, each having ten syllables.

The verse below, which is the first verse of the second epistle, begins by setting out the main lesson Pope wants readers to learn from his poem:

Know then thyself, presume not God to scan;
The proper study of mankind is man.

Although these lines are often quoted, few realize that they are a summary of Pope's overall purpose, which was to show that everything does, in fact, make good sense, so we can believe the world to be God's good creation. He argues that we cannot know God's purpose in particular events and we have to accept that our tiny human minds are very limited, as well as being liable to error. What we can do, however, is look at human beings and, when we do that, we can see how all the features of our lives have a purpose which relates to the kind of creatures we are.

Also, as we survey the universe, we cannot know whether there are other worlds where God is known or not, but what we do know is what it is to be human and, as such, part of a much larger whole. In the great chain of being, there are many forms of life and the only question is, do we have a form of life that is appropriate to our status? We can think only in terms of single, limited goals, but God is not so constrained and may have a further purpose for us. As the poem continues:

So man, who here seems principal alone,
Perhaps acts second to some sphere unknown,
Touches some wheel, or verges to some goal;
'Tis but a part we see, and not a whole.

Just as a horse does not know exactly what its rider's plans are, nor do we know God's. We must therefore accept that the mixed fortunes of our lives are the right ones for our state. For example, it is for our good that we do not know what fate has in store for us. As Pope notes, would the lamb gambol in the field if it knew it was due to be killed?

We are, he says, to 'hope humbly' that all will become clear. 'Hope springs eternal in the breast.' We use our minds to judge God, but that is to invert the natural order of things. As Pope goes on to say, we think of nature existing for our benefit, but it doesn't; it operates according to natural laws:

No, ('tis replied) the first Almighty Cause
Acts not by partial, but by gen'ral laws;
. . .
Everything in nature has a special instinct
. . .
The spider's touch, how exquisitely fine!
Feels at each thread, and lives along the line:
In the nice bee, what sense so subtly true
From pois'nous herbs extracts the healing dew?

In the same way, our bodies are just right for us, and we have the great gift of reason. Humans occupy their appropriate place in the great chain of being. It is simply pride to question that:

All are but parts of one stupendous whole,
Whose body Nature is, and God the soul.

Pope compares the world to a work of art that is in progress. He argues that it has a direction, even though, as we are part of the work itself, we are not in a position to know what it is now:

All nature is but art, unknown to thee;
All chance, direction, which thou canst not see.

Pope also argues that science is good, but it still provides us with only a limited knowledge of the whole, so science needs to be done modestly.

Trace science then, with modesty thy guide;
First strip off all her equipage of pride.

Particularly interesting is Pope's insight that our virtues are so often mixed up with our vices, so:

As fruits, ungrateful to the planter's care,
On savage stocks inserted, learn to bear;
The surest virtues thus from passions shoot,
Wild nature's vigor working at the root.
What crops of wit and honesty appear
From spleen, from obstinacy, hate, or fear!

All this poetic work of Christian apology – that is, justifying the ways of God to human beings – is designed to bear out the opening lines with which we started: there is a proper agnosticism concerning God and his ways and 'the proper study of mankind is man'. If we use our reason to do this, we can see that the world is fit for the purpose of creating rational, moral beings like us.

Thursday
Eve remembering

Toni Morrison

1

I tore from a limb fruit that had lost its green.
My hands were warmed by the heat of an apple
Fire red and humming.
I bit sweet power to the core.
How can I say what it was like?
The taste! The taste undid my eyes
And led me far from the gardens planted for a child
To wildernesses deeper than any master's call.

2

Now these cool hands guide what they once caressed;
Lips forget what they have kissed.
My eyes now pool their light
Better the summit to see.

3

I would do it all over again:
Be the harbour and set the sail,
Loose the breeze and harness the gale,
Cherish the harvest of what I have been.
Better the summit to scale.
Better the summit to be.

Toni Morrison (1931–2019)

Toni Morrison's working-class family originally came from the state of Georgia. To escape the lynching there, they moved to the more racially integrated Ohio, but there too they encountered extreme prejudice. The landlord of their house tried to burn it down when they failed to pay the rent on time. The family simply laughed at this crass gesture.

Chloe Wofford, as she was then, read widely from the time she was young and also learned African stories and myths from her mother, who was a devout member of the African Methodist Episcopal Church. She herself became a Roman Catholic at the age of 12. She adopted the baptismal name of Anthony of Padua, hence the name by which she is known now: Toni.

Educated at Howard University, Morrison went on to study at Cornell and later held a number of prestigious teaching positions. At the same time, she was a highly influential editor at Random House. She wrote many novels, of which *The Beloved* is the best-known title. She was awarded numerous prizes, including the Pulitzer Prize and the Nobel Prize in Literature. She became a much loved iconic figure for millions.

In the above poem, Eve is like no other portrayal of the wife of Adam. Instead of shyly taking the apple from the tree, she tears it off and warms her hands on the red skin. Eating it to the core, she tastes sweet power. Her eyes are opened and she is led to the deep future that beckons. Far from feeling remorse for what she has done, she would do it again. She exults in setting sail on the voyage of life, gales and all. With no regrets, Eve cherishes what she has been and now feels better able to climb what lies ahead. She relishes being herself, taking power into her own hands and taking responsibility for her life. She will herself be a summit.

Much traditional interpretation of the garden of Eden story sees Eve's eating of the apple as disobedience and the beginning of sin, which has tainted humankind ever since. It was essential, though, for us to grow out of the dreaming innocence of Eden and take responsibility for our own lives. This capacity, this power, is a gift from God, and it is one in which Morrison exults.

Friday
One foot in Eden still, I stand
Edwin Muir

Yet still from Eden springs the root
As clean as on the starting day.
Time takes the foliage and the fruit
And burns the archetypal leaf
To shapes of terror and of grief
Scattered along the winter way.
But famished field and blackened tree
Bear flowers in Eden never known.
Blossoms of grief and charity
Bloom in these darkened fields alone.
What had Eden ever to say
Of hope and faith and pity and love
And memory found its treasure trove?
Strange blessings never in Paradise
Fall from these beclouded skies.

Edwin Muir (1887–1959)

For the first 14 years of his life, Edwin Muir lived in the Orkneys, then, as a result of poverty, the family had to move to Glasgow. It felt to him like being expelled from the garden of Eden, and the thought of Eden haunted him all his life. It is fundamental to this poem. He was further devastated when, on a tram one day, all the passengers seemed to be only animals on the way to a slaughterhouse. After this sense of total disenchantment, Muir gradually, over the course of his life, rediscovered a sense of the spiritual in human beings.

Muir had a successful career at the British Council, serving as its head in Prague and, later, in Rome. At the same time, he established a high reputation as a poet. In Rome, he encountered images of the Christian faith, such as the annunciation, about which he wrote a lovely poem, and this made him rethink the Christian faith in which he had been brought up. As a child, Muir had encountered a religion of the word, but nothing told him that Christ had been born in the flesh.

A religion that dared to show forth the mystery for everyone to see would have shocked the congregations of the North, and would have seemed a sort of blasphemy, perhaps even indecent, but here it was publicly shown, as Christ showed himself on earth: 'This open declaration was to me the very mark of Christianity, distinguishing it from the older religions. For although the pagan gods had visited the earth, they did not assume the burden of our flesh, live our life and die our death.'[19]

In the first verse of this poem, not quoted here, Muir is still conscious of having one foot in Eden, but the world he experiences now is full of hate as well as love. Drawing on the image of the parable of Jesus about the wheat and the tares, he knows that good and evil cannot be separated in this world; we have to look to the harvest for the weeds to be pulled out. But, as he continues in this second verse, the world, at its root, is still good. Life in time brings grief but also the kind of love that could not exist in a world of dreaming innocence. Hope, faith, pity and love were simply not known in that world, but bloom in these darkened fields alone, so:

Strange blessings never in Paradise
Fall from these beclouded skies.

We have to be careful here not to suggest that God created the world with its horrors in order to bring about these spiritual goods. Rather, God created the world we have because it is the only kind of world that allows for the emergence of genuine autonomy and free choice, which means that natural disasters and wrongdoing are an inescapable fact of life. Nevertheless, that said, God is ceaselessly at work drawing good out of evil, which leads to the highest and most worthwhile of human qualities, such as pity and love.

I think Muir got it right when, at the end of his autobiography, he reflects on his own periods of depression. He wrote:

Now and then during the years I fell into the dumps for short or prolonged periods, was subject to fears which I did not understand, and passed through stretches of blankness and deprivation. From these I learned things which I could not otherwise have learned, so that I cannot regard them as mere loss. Yet I believe that I would have been better without them.[20]

I love that statement, with its understated pain and honesty. Muir did not have an easy life and, in one poem, 'The desolations', he writes about his depression in terms of desolations. He knew what it was like to live with 'famished field and blackened tree'. He would rather not have gone through all that, yet he recognized that, without them, his insight into life would have been the poorer.[21]

Saturday
Who am I?

Dietrich Bonhoeffer

Who am I? They often tell me
I would step from my cell's confinement
calmly, cheerfully, firmly,
like a squire from his country house.
Who am I? They often tell me
I would talk to my warders
freely and friendly and clearly,
as though it were mine to command.
Who am I? They also tell me
I would bear the days of misfortune
equably, smilingly, proudly,
like one accustomed to win.

Am I then really all that which other men tell of?
Or am I only what I know of myself,
restless and longing and sick, like a bird in a cage,
struggling for breath, as though hands were compressing
    my throat,
yearning for colours, for flowers, for the voices of birds,
thirsting for words of kindness, for neighbourliness,
trembling with anger at despotisms and petty humiliation,
tossing in expectation of great events,
powerlessly trembling for friends at an infinite distance,
weary and empty at praying, at thinking, at making;
faint, and ready to say farewell to it all?

Who am I? This or the other?
Am I one person today, and tomorrow another?
Am I both at once? A hypocrite before others,
and before myself a contemptibly woebegone weakling?
Or is something within me still like a beaten army,
fleeing in disorder from victory already achieved?

Who am I? They mock me, these lonely questions of mine.
Whoever I am, thou knowest, O God, I am thine.

Dietrich Bonhoeffer (1906–1945)

Bonhoeffer grew up in a highly educated family at the heart of Berlin's cultural elite. Ordained in the German Lutheran Church, he quickly made a name for himself as a promising theologian – one clearly influenced by Karl Barth. When the Nazis came to power, he saw the danger and called the Church to a more costly following of Christ, accusing it of preaching 'cheap grace'. Then, when the Nazis passed laws forbidding people of Jewish background to hold office in the Church, he, in cooperation with others, founded the Confessing Church. He rightly regarded this law as totally incompatible with the Christian faith. Bonhoeffer himself ran a small seminary for pastors of this Church where he tried to build a Christian community. Out of this experience, he wrote the spiritual classic *Life Together*. In 1939, he went to America but, after two weeks, decided to return because, as he wrote to the great American theologian Reinhold Niebuhr:

> Christians in Germany will have to face the terrible alternative of either willing the defeat of their nation in order that Christian civilization may survive or willing the victory of their nation and thereby destroying civilization. I know which of these alternatives I must choose but I cannot make that choice from security.[22]

Bonhoeffer was imprisoned in 1943 and when, in 1944, the 20 June plot to assassinate Hitler failed, he was implicated and hanged, shortly before the end of the war. He told his friends, 'This is the end. For me the beginning of life.'

In prison, he wrote a number of letters subsequently published as *Letters and Papers from Prison*, which were to be highly influential in the 1960s, arguing for a new form of Christianity appropriate to a secular age. This book also contained prayers and poems, of which the above is one.

'Who am I?' expresses Bonhoeffer's anguished, conflicting thoughts in prison. Outwardly, he seemed so calm and brave. Inwardly, he knew himself to be sick and fearful. He wonders which is the real person – the one others see or the person he feels he is inside. Then he reflects that perhaps he is both at once. He ends with two wonderful lines, at once both knowing nothing and full of faith:

Who am I? They mock me, these lonely questions of mine.
Whoever I am, thou knowest, O God, I am thine.

Bonhoeffer does not know which is the real him, but he is certain that God does, and, whoever he is, he knows that he belongs to God.

HOLY WEEK
DEATH

Monday
When my time come

Khadijah Ibrahiim

'The lord is my shepherd I shall not want,
He maketh me to lie down in green pastures'

– Psalm 23

Mi dear chile,
we are livin' in our last days,
so when mi time come,
I waant to be buried in mi red suit,
the one I just buy.

I buy a new one every five years
just for de occasion,
I like to keep with the fashion
and dis suit favour de roses in my garden –
you know how I love dem so.

So look here, child,
when mi time come I waant you
to remember
dis is de suit I waant to be buried in,
de red one right here,
trailing from neck to hem
wid beads and silk embroidery
just like royalty,
a colour of importance.

Holy Week: Death

I saw de queen wearing one just like it pon TV.
So remember wat mi show you;
see how it tailor stitched in and out
with good threads,
like mi granny use to do.
She bury in red too.

And when de Lord calls
I want to be wearing a red suit,
de one I handpick especially –
I walk de whole day till carn bun mi toes.

I like to look good at all times,
no-one is going to say
I never dress away till de end of my days.
Mi buy mi suit from Marks and Spencer,
all mi underwear too,
put dem in de trunk
with all mi fine nightwear and tings,
fold in camphor balls.
Mi a ole woman, 75 years just gone,
but mi a no fool,
mi make all mi plans;
put down insurance
fe horse-drawn carriage,
gospel singers, saxophone player,
and a red rose for each and every one.

Mi no waant bury a England,
mi waant mi ashes spread cross de River
Thames, make de waves teck
mi back to which part mi did come from.

And when all and sundries come to the house,
start dig, stake claim to what dem waant,
to wat dem no waant,
when tears flare and tongues clash difference,
I want my daughter to remember
dis is the red suit I waant to be buried in,

the red one, right here.

Khadijah Ibrahiim

Khadijah Ibrahiim was born in Leeds and has an MA in Theatre
Studies from the University of Leeds. A theatre-maker (which is to
create theatre through performance – writing from page to stage) as
well as a poet and researcher, she is Artistic Director of Leeds Young
Authors and the producer of the Leeds youth poetry slam festival.
She is currently working with Opera North.

Ibrahiim is of Jamaican heritage; her latest volume of poetry, *Another Crossing*, celebrates the life of her family and community, past
and present, with joy and vibrancy. She has toured international-
ly with her work and is regarded as one of Yorkshire's leading poets.

I love the individual voice that comes across in the poem above:
it is forceful, definite, not to be mucked about. The poem is about
Khadijah's grandmother, a powerful figure around whom the rest
of the family revolved, and with whom she spent much of her child-
hood. She was a woman who had a very strong belief in a life be-
yond death, and definite views about how she wanted to be cremated.
Khadijah is herself researching the different burial customs of the
very varied communities in Jamaica.

From the earliest days, people have wanted to be buried with ar-
ticles that have meant a lot to them, that express who they are and
that (in the beliefs of many cultures) would be of use to them in
the hereafter. Much archaeological work is based upon what these
grave goods reveal about the deceased and their communities. This

instinct is still present today. The Revd Richard Coles, the broadcaster, describes how when his partner, also a priest, died, he was buried according to his wishes with the apparel and insignia of priesthood. Others have gone to their graves with items such as a cricket bat (reflecting their life-long passion), a teddy bear or other favourite object. They wanted to say something about who they were or what was important to them.

The owner of the poetic voice in Khadijah Ibrahiim's piece is quite clear that she wants to go to her grave in her favourite red suit. The colour red is important. It is bright and bold; it says: 'This is me and I'm glad to be me.' It also says: 'I want to look my best.' The poem brought to my mind the death of a friend, another larger-than-life person; one of those people around whom everything happened and everything was lively. Lying in a hospital bed and told she had only a very short time to live, she quickly retorted: 'Then bring me my brightest red lipstick.' It was characteristic of her whole approach to life.

The poem does, of course, raise wider questions about how we want to appear at the end of our lives, not just in the way we look but also in who we are as individuals; about how we want to be remembered by others – and how we want to present ourselves before God.

Tuesday
The trees are down

Charlotte Mew

– and he cried with a loud voice:
Hurt not the earth, neither the sea, nor the trees –
(Revelation)

They are cutting down the great plane-trees at the end of
    the gardens.
For days there has been the grate of the saw, the swish of
    the branches as they fall,
The crash of the trunks, the rustle of trodden leaves,
With the 'Whoops' and the 'Whoas,' the loud common
    talk, the loud common laughs of the men, above it all.

I remember one evening of a long past spring
Turning in at a gate, getting out of a cart, and finding a
    large dead rat in the mud of the drive.
I remember thinking: alive or dead, a rat was a god-
    forsaken thing,
But at least, in May, that even a rat should be alive.

The week's work here is as good as done. There is just one
    bough
  On the roped bole, in the fine grey rain,
      Green and high
      And lonely against the sky.
        (Down now! –)

And but for that,
If an old dead rat
Did once, for a moment, unmake the spring, I might never
have thought of him again.

It is not for a moment the spring is unmade to-day;
These were great trees, it was in them from root to stem:
When the men with the 'Whoops' and the 'Whoas' have
carted the whole of the whispering loveliness away
Half the spring, for me, will have gone with them.

It is going now, and my heart has been struck with the
hearts of the planes;
Half my life it has beat with these, in the sun, in the rains,
In the March wind, the May breeze,
In the great gales that came over to them across the roofs
from the great seas.
There was only a quiet rain when they were dying;
They must have heard the sparrows flying,
And the small creeping creatures in the earth where they
were lying –
But I, all day, I heard an angel crying:
'Hurt not the trees.'

Charlotte Mew (1869–1928)

Charlotte Mew did not have an easy life. When her father died, the family was left with very little money. Three of her siblings died young and two were committed to mental asylums. For this reason, she and her remaining sister vowed not to marry. Charlotte was a lesbian, but her approaches to other women were never reciprocated. When her sister died, she went into a deep depression and committed suicide.

Mew's life straddled very different periods, from high Victorian to modernist. In the early part of her life, she wrote articles and short stories and only later did she turn to poetry. The quality of this was quickly recognized by people such as Thomas Hardy and Virginia Woolf, who thought her the best female poet of the age. The critical estimate of her remains high, though she still deserves to be better known.

This poem, with its heartfelt anguish over nature, is very much one for our own time. Gerald Manley Hopkins had a similar anguish, expressed not only in such lines as 'Long live the weeds and the wilderness yet' in 'Inversnaid' but also in the poem he wrote about the felling of the poplar trees in Binsey.

Many of us feel that there is something very special about trees, and this is recognized in Revelation 7.3, which Charlotte Mew quotes as a heading to the poem. London's plane trees, most of which were planted in the eighteenth and nineteenth centuries, remain one of the glories of the city. Mew contrasts the grandeur and stillness of the plane trees with the rough shouts of those cutting them down. It is just one sign of a wider anguish, the limited life of everything on earth. She remembers a dead rat she saw one spring. Even a rat, she thinks, deserves to be alive to enjoy the vitality of spring.

The felling of the planes has also spoiled her spring but, with the planes, it is not just one spring that has been spoiled. Those planes had been part of her life. St Paul wrote about this anguish of nature in Romans 8.18–24: 'the whole created universe in all its parts groans' (REB). There he expresses the hope that when the new creation, of which we are the first fruits, comes to its fulfilment, nature itself will be transformed: 'the universe itself is to be freed from the shackles of mortality and is to enter upon the glorious liberty of the children of God' (v. 21, REB). Meanwhile, we are now highly conscious of the preciousness of nature and the need to preserve it from human degradation, climate change and the loss of biodiversity. Trees in the UK are not in a good state. One of our glories, the ash, has been totally devastated in just a few years by ash dieback. This follows the virtual end of the English elm several decades ago.

The oak and the chestnut are also being blighted by disease. At the same time, we know that there is a desperate need to plant more trees in order to absorb some of the carbon dioxide in the atmosphere, which has been contributing to global warming and climate change. With Charlotte Mew, echoing the book of Revelation, we cry out, 'Hurt not the trees.'

Wednesday
The father, the son

Roger McGough

It is unusual to find me here, in town.
I never did like crowds. The smell,
The dust, the racket. I can do without it.
But it's a special occasion, and well,
I haven't seen him in a long, long time.

Followed his career with interest, mind.
Well, hardly career, but he's made his mark
They all have, and good on them I say.
The whole country needs shaking up
And they're the boys to do it.

Things are coming to a head now.
History in the making, you can sense it.
That's why I am here. I may be old
But not too old to lend a hand
Lift a sword and strike a blow for freedom.

[The poem then goes on to lament the corruption that
        might ruin everything.]

Unless this Jesus can provide the glue
By all accounts he knows a thing or two.
Peace is what he preaches. A coded message

That's clear to understand: There'll be no peace
Until Rome has been driven from this land.

And my son knows that. That's why
He got involved. To fight for the cause.
A chip off the block and no mistake.
But smarter. Not like his old man, hot-headed.
He likes to plan. Take stock. Cool in a crisis.

Ah, there's something happening now.
You can hear the cheering? It must be them.
The crowd is ecstatic, and the soldiers,
Under orders, keeping out of the way.
Nervous too, a good sign that, I'd say.

But where's my lad? Ah, there he is
At the back, following at a slower pace.
Looks strangely downcast, I must confess.
But no doubt the sight of his old dad
Will bring a smile to his face . . .
'Judas! . . . Judas!'

Roger McGough (born 1937)

Roger McGough, of Irish descent, was born and brought up on the
outskirts of Liverpool. After education in Roman Catholic schools,
he studied French at the University of Hull and then returned to
Merseyside to teach. Part of the Liverpool scene in the 1960s, he
had success as a writer of lyrics, sketches and poems. One group
of which he was a member reached No. 1 in the UK singles chart
in 1968. *The Mersey Sound*, a collection of poems by him and two
other Liverpool poets, Brian Patten and Adrian Henri, published in
1967, sold half a million copies – one of the bestselling anthologies
of all time. A friend of the Beatles, McGough wrote much of the

humorous dialogue of the animated film *The Yellow Submarine*, but did not receive an onscreen credit. He has also translated three plays by Molière.

McGough has a vast *oeuvre* in a variety of forms and is pre-senter of BBC Radio 4's *Poetry Please*. Described by Carol Ann Duffy as 'The Patron Saint of Poetry', he is unusual in having both wide popular appeal and being appreciated by literary critics. His style is jaunty, colloquial and full of the wit and humour for which Liver-pool is famous.

The poem above catches a very particular colloquial voice: that of a fairly rough father, not close to his son, but interested to see how he has made out. He comes to Jerusalem because he has heard his son is part of a group creating something of a stir. The country certainly needs it, for it is under an oppressive occupation by the Romans, as well as being full of the usual rogues and villains who could spoil the whole thing. Perhaps this new leader can mould it into a real force for change? Then he spots his son and calls out, 'Judas!'

No reader can come to the end of this poem without being shaken. All the early verses serve to build up a great sense of expectation, and then we find that the father's own son is the betrayer. The father does not know this, but we the readers know it. We are jolted into realiz-ing that Judas is not just a cardboard cut-out figure. He had a father and a mother who, in their way, loved him. The mystery of why Judas betrayed Jesus remains. The mystery of what was in him that made him do it is also hidden. As another poet, the Irishman George Wil-liam Russell, who published under the pseudonym Æ, wrote, 'In the lost boyhood of Judas, Christ was betrayed.'

Maundy Thursday
The Dream of the Rood
Early English, anonymous

Many years ago – the memory abides –
I was felled to the ground at the forest's edge,
Severed from my roots. Enemies seized me,
Made of me a mark of scorn for criminals to mount on;
Shoulder-high they carried me and set me on a hill.
Many foes made me fast there. Far off then I saw
The King of all mankind coming in great haste,
With courage keen, eager to climb me . . .
Then the young Hero – it was God almighty –
Strong and steadfast, stripped himself for battle;
He climbed up on high gallows, constant in his purpose,
Mounted it in sight of many, mankind to ransom.
Horror seized me when the Hero clasped me,
But I dared not bow or bend down to earth.
Nor falter, nor fall; firm I needs must stand.
I was raised up a Rood,* a royal King I bore,
The High King of Heaven: hold firm I must.
They drove dark nails through me, the dire wounds still
          show,
Cruel, gaping gashes, yet I dared not give as good.
They taunted the two of us; I was wet with teeming blood,

---

*'Rood' means rod or pole and, hence, came to mean the wooden cross. So it is that the rood screen in a church is the screen between the sanctuary and the nave on which a crucifix is hung.

Streaming from the warrior's side when he sent forth his
    spirit.
High upon a hill helpless I suffered
Long hours of torment; I saw the Lord of hosts
Outstretched in agony; all embracing darkness
Covered with thick clouds the corpse of the World's Ruler,
The bright day was darkened by a deep shadow,
All its colours clouded; the whole creation wept,
Keened for its King's fall; Christ was on the Rood.
Yet warriors from afar eagerly came speeding
To where he hung alone. All this I beheld.

In the fourth century, Helena, the mother of the Roman emperor Constantine, travelled from the North of England to Jerusalem. Constantine, had newly converted to Christianity and, according to legend, Helena set about locating the places associated with Christ's life and death. She discovered the site where Christ was crucified and the cross on which he was hung and also the site where he was buried. A church was erected at the site, the Church of the Holy Sepulchre. In due course, a large cross was erected outside the church, encased in metal with protruding jewels and studs.

Over the centuries, pilgrims came from all over the world to visit the church and took back with them not only holy souvenirs but also the memory of that cross. Back in their own countries, they erected replicas of it as a witness and sign of the victory of Christ over pagan darkness. Many of those high crosses, dating from the seventh to the twelfth centuries, can be seen in Ireland today. They are carved from stone and, in addition to showing scenes from the life of Christ, they clearly show the influence of that cross outside the Church of the Holy Sepulchre.[23]

One of the crosses, dating from the seventh century, can be seen in Ruthwell, now in Scotland but originally in Northumbria. This has inscriptions on it in Latin, plus Anglo-Saxon runes. The runes,

139

which may be later than the cross itself, are lines that are also part of *The Dream of the Rood*. This poem is preserved in the tenth-century Vercelli document, named after the town in Italy where it is kept, and is one of the very earliest English poems. Although some scholars have tried to attribute it to known Christian poets of the time, such as Caedmon, their reasons have not convinced the majority.

The first part of the poem describes how someone in a dream saw a most beautiful cross:

> It seemed to me that I saw a more wonderful tree
> Lifted in the air, wound round with light,
> The brightest of beams. That beacon was entirely
> Cased in gold. Beautiful gems stood
> At the corners of the earth, likewise there were five
> upon the cross beam. All those fair through creation
> gazed on the angel of the Lord there.

We note that the description of the cross is very like the stone ones still to be seen that were based on the prototype in Jerusalem. The poem then switches its voice so it is no longer that of the dreamer but the cross itself, as in the part of the poem quoted above. The final part of the poem, which is some 156 lines, describes the resurrection and the Lord, now acknowledged as the true King, giving a great banquet for his followers.

In the part of the poem quoted above, the cross remembers when he was once a tree in a forest and was cut down to make a scaffold for criminals. Then how he saw the King of humankind not being thrust on to the cross but eager to climb on him like a hero going into battle. He remembers the terrible pain the King had to go through in order to ransom humanity, and he sees himself as a faithful retainer, suffering with his Lord. The poem uses the imagery of the time it was written, that of the heroic warrior king to depict Christ, with the cross as his trusty servant. Both fight bravely in the battle and, though killed, are victorious in the struggle against evil.

Finally, the dreamer says that his great hope is to look on the cross and prove worthy of it.

And I myself hope
each day for when the Lord's cross,
that I looked at here on earth,
will fetch me from this transitory life,
and then bring me where there is great bliss,
joy in heaven, where the Lord's people
are set in feasting, where there is unceasing bliss;
and then will set me where I might afterwards
dwell in glory fully with the saints
to partake of joy. May the Lord be a friend to me.

Good Friday
To the good thief

Saunders Lewis

You did not see Him on the mountain of Transfiguration
Nor walking the sea at night;
You never saw corpses blushing when a bier or sepulchre
Was stuck by his cry.

It was in the rawness of his flesh and his dirt that you saw
     Him,
Whipped and under thorns,
And in his nailing like a sack of bones outside the town
On a pole, like a scarecrow.

You never heard the making of the parables like a Parthenon
     of words,
Nor his tone when He talked of his father,
Neither did you hear the secrets of the room above,
Nor the prayer before Cedron and the treachery.

It was in the racket of a crowd of sadists revelling in pain
And their screeches, howls, curses, and shouts
That you heard the profound cry of the breaking heart of
     their prey:
'Why hast thou forsaken me?'

You, hanging on his right; on his left, your brother;
Writhing like skinned frogs,

Flea-bitten petty thieves thrown in as a retinue to his
      shame,
Courtiers to a mock king in his pain.

O master of courtesy and manners, who enlightened you
About your part in this harsh parody?
'Lord, when you come into your kingdom, remember me,' –
The kingdom that was conquered through death.

Rex Judaeorum; it was you who saw first the vain
Blasphemy as a living oracle,
You who first believed in the Latin, Hebrew and Greek,
That the gallows was the throne of God.

O thief who took Paradise from the nails of a gibbet,
Foremost of the nobilitas of heaven,
Before the hour of death pray that it may be given to us
To perceive Him and to taste Him.

Saunders Lewis (1893–1985)

Saunders Lewis was educated at the University of Liverpool and served
in the South Wales Borderers in the First World War, during which
time he was wounded. It was while he was in the army that his interest
in nationalism was aroused, and he was one of the founders of Plaid
Cymru in 1925, later becoming its president. Throughout his life, he
was a controversial figure, never fitting happily into the party, because
of his sometimes right-wing views, his unrealistic aims or extreme
tactics, but the results of a poll on St David's Day in 2004 placed him
tenth on a list of 100 greatest Welsh people. Lewis's great aim, he said,
was to 'rescue Wales from political and cultural oblivion'. In order to
achieve that, first it was necessary to stop the decline of the Welsh lan-
guage. That was fundamental, so he worked with others to get Welsh
programmes on the BBC at a time when this was forbidden.

Regarded as one of the great Welsh literary figures of the twentieth century, Lewis wrote plays, novels and poetry. He became a Roman Catholic in 1932 – one of the reasons, in a Methodist Calvinist culture, his leadership of Plaid Cymru was considered problematical. Lewis's vision, however, was for a Welsh-speaking, independent nation, proud of its ancient culture, within the European Union.

The poem above, originally written in Welsh in 1939 as 'I'r lleidr da', is based on the famous incident described in Luke 23.39–43. It begins by pointing out that the thief had no chance to see Jesus glorified in the transfiguration, performing his miracles, hearing his teaching or hearing him pray. It was in the racket made by sadists that he heard the cry of his heart breaking. Then, in the last three verses, the whole tone changes and creates a scene like a medieval court. The thief is a 'master of courtesy and manners', 'foremost of the nobilitas of heaven'. That is because he was the first to see the gallows as the throne of God, the first to recognize the cruel irony of 'King of the Jews' as divine irony, for Christ is indeed King of kings. So it is the poet asks that we too may perceive him and taste him.

Holy Saturday
No coward soul is mine

Emily Brontë

No coward soul is mine
No trembler in the world's storm-troubled sphere
I see Heaven's glories shine
And Faith shines equal arming me from Fear

O God within my breast
Almighty ever-present Deity
Life, that in me hast rest,
As I Undying Life, have power in Thee

Vain are the thousand creeds
That move men's hearts, unutterably vain,
Worthless as withered weeds
Or idlest froth amid the boundless main

To waken doubt in one
Holding so fast by thy infinity,
So surely anchored on
The steadfast rock of Immortality.

With wide-embracing love
Thy spirit animates eternal years
Pervades and broods above,
Changes, sustains, dissolves, creates and rears

Though earth and moon were gone
And suns and universes ceased to be
And Thou wert left alone
Every Existence would exist in thee

There is not room for Death
Nor atom that his might could render void
Since thou art Being and Breath
And what thou art may never be destroyed.

Emily Brontë (1818–1848)

Emily Brontë was one of six children born to a poor clergyman of Irish stock who served the parish of Haworth in Yorkshire. Their mother died when all the children were under the age of eight, and Emily was only three, so they were brought up by relatives. From an early age, the children wrote elaborate fantasy stories and poems that stretched their imagination and honed their writing skills. Three of the children became famous as authors: Charlotte whose novel *Jane Eyre* found instant success; Ann, who died at 29 having published *Agnes Grey* and *The Tenant of Wildfell Hall*; and Emily, whose novel *Wuthering Heights* was not well received at the time but which is now regarded as a classic of English fiction. The three women also wrote a collection of poems together, published, like their novels, under pseudonyms. Emily Brontë studied in Brussels and was fluent in German and French, but was too fragile to pursue the teaching career she had planned. She died at the age of 30 before her work achieved its recognition.

Emily Brontë was a solitary child and all who met her remarked on her fierce independence of mind and character, even wildness. That force emerges clearly in this poem, which begins by defiant-ly asserting the primacy of faith over fear. She goes on to affirm the presence of God within her that, she asserts, cannot be shaken by the variety of religious creeds, which she regards as worthless. Her belief, like that of Emily Dickinson later, was founded on the rock of immortality. In the last verses, she affirms the ground of this conviction, which is not that she is immortal in herself, but God is; and even if all dissolved and disappeared, she would exist, as would everything else, lodged, as we might say, in the heart and mind of God. God is an immortal being and breath, and what lives in him can never be destroyed.

EASTER AND
INTO THE NEW
LIFE IN CHRIST

Easter Day
Piers Plowman (Passus XVIII)
William Langland

Christ's descent into hell to rescue the departed

'I may do mercy through righteousness · and all my words
    true.
And though holy writ wills that I be avenged · on them that
    did ill,

Nullum malum impunitum, etc.

They shall be cleansed clearly · and washed of their sins
In my prison Purgatory · till *parce* is called,
And my mercy shall be showed · to many of my bretheren.
For blood may suffer blood · both hungry and a'cold,
But blood may not see blood · bleed, without pity.

Audivi arcana verba, quae non licet homini loqui.

But my righteousness and right · shall rule all Hell,
And mercy all mankind · before me in Heaven.
For I were an unkind king · unless I my kindred helped,
And above all at such need · when help needs must come;

Non intres in judicium cum servo tuo, Domine.

Thus by law,' quoth our Lord · 'lead I will from hence
Those that me loved · and believed in my coming.
And for thy lying, Lucifer · that thou told to Eve,
Thou shalt abide it bitterly' · and bound him with chains.
Ashtoreth and all the rout · hid them in corners,
They dared not look on our Lord · the boldest of them
    all,
But let him lead forth what he liked · and allowed him what
    he pleased.
Many hundreds of angels · harped and sung,
Culpat caro, purgat caro; regnat Deus Dei caro.

Then piped Peace · of poesy a note,

'Clarior est solito post maxima nebula Phoebus,
Post inimicitias clarior est et amor.

After sharp showers,' quoth Peace · 'most glorious is the
    sun;
Is no weather warmer · than after watery clouds.
Nor no love dearer · nor dearer friends,
Than after war and woe · when Love and Peace be masters.
Was never war in this world · nor wickedness so keen,
That Love, if he pleased · could not bring to laughter,
And Peace through patience · all perils stopped.'
'Truce,' quoth Truth · 'thou tellest us soth, by Jesus.
Clip we in covenant · and each of us kiss the other!'
'And let no people,' quoth Peace · 'perceive that we chid?
For impossible is no thing · to him that is almighty.'
'Thou sayest soth,' said Righteousness · and reverently her
    kissed,
Peace, and Peace her · *per saecula saeculorum.*

*Misericordia et veritas obviaverunt sibi; justitia et pax
osculatae sunt.*

Truth trumpeted then, and sang · '*Te Deum laudamus*'[24]

William Langland (c.1332–c.1386)

William Langland is the presumed author of *Piers Plowman*. Almost nothing is known about him except that he lived in the West Midlands. Anything we do know is derived from this poem, which is attributed to him on the grounds of the internal evidence of the poem itself.

Written in unrhymed alliterative verse, it is regarded as one of the two greatest poems in Middle English and was an influence on Chaucer. It is a mix of theological allegory and social satire and concerns the narrator/dreamer's quest for the true Christian life. This journey takes place within a series of dream-visions concerning Do well, Do better and Do best.

The part of the poem given above describes Christ's descent into hell in order to rescue the souls imprisoned there. In 1 Peter 3.18–20, we read that Christ 'preached unto the spirits in prison; which sometime were disobedient' (vv. 19–20, KJV). In about AD 600, the *Gospel of Nicodemus* appeared, elaborating on that lapidary verse. It describes how Joseph of Arimathea summoned the two sons of Simeon to witness to what happened in hell after Christ's resurrection. The text was highly influential in shaping the icon of the Anastasis, the mystery plays and this poem.[25]

In the above poem, the two sons describe how a great light shone in the darkness and Psalm 24 was sung exultantly: 'Lift up your heads, O ye gates . . . and the King of glory shall come in' (vv. 7 and 9, KJV) Then Christ broke down the doors and led out formerly doomed humanity. In the excerpt above, Christ says that he will have mercy on those in purgatory, 'For I were an unkind king unless I my

kindred helped.' So Christ leads out the redeemed to general rejoic-
ing for there was never wickedness so appalling:

> That Love, if he pleased · could not bring to laughter,
> And Peace through patience · all perils stopped.

If we doubt this, the answer comes, 'For impossible is no thing · to
him that is almighty.'

Monday of Easter Week
Easter

Edmund Spenser

MOST glorious Lord of Life! that, on this day,
Didst make Thy triumph over death and sin;
And, having harrowed hell, didst bring away
Captivity thence captive, us to win:
This joyous day, dear Lord, with joy begin;
And grant that we, for whom thou didst die,
Being with Thy dear blood clean washed from sin,
May live for ever in felicity!

And that Thy love we weighing worthily,
May likewise love Thee for the same again;
And for Thy sake, that all like dear didst buy
With love may one another entertain!
   So let us love, dear Love, like as we ought,
   Love is the lesson which the Lord us taught.

Edmund Spenser (1552/3–1599)

Edmund Spenser came from a modest background, but received
a good education at Merchant Taylors' School and Cambridge. He
then went into service with the English government in Ireland,
where he stayed and purchased land. His passion, however, was po-
etry and he wrote one of the longest poems in the English language,
The Faerie Queene, in celebration of the Tudor dynasty and Queen
Elizabeth (Queen Gloriana) in particular. For this, he was awarded
a pension of £50 a year.

Spenser wrote 89 sonnets under the heading 'Amoretti' – literally little loves or cupids – for his second wife (his first wife died). The above poem is the sixty-eighth poem in that sequence. Spenser invented a sonnet form of his own, slightly different from those of both Petrarch and Shakespeare, in both its meter and rhyming scheme, as we see in this example. He has been very highly regarded by poets in every generation and has sometimes been called 'the poet's poet'. His views in support of the Protestant rule in Ireland were totally unacceptable and, not surprisingly, his castle was burnt to the ground and he returned to England. According to Ben Jonson, one of Spenser's children was lost in the fire. He died at the age of 46 'for want of bread', a statement regarded as doubtful.

Rather surprisingly, there are very few good poems on the resurrection of Christ, but this one is brilliant, in terms of both its affirmation and its joy. It is very accessible without being sentimental or simplistic. It started appearing in hymn books to the tune of Farley Castle in 1875 and has been set to music by a number of composers since, including John Rutter.

The very first line, with its reference to the 'Lord of Life', lifts the heart and, after the agony of Holy Week, it celebrates a great triumph. Taking up the image of the descent into hell or harrowing of hell discussed in the previous section, it draws on the imagery of St Paul in Ephesians 4.8: all that held us captive is itself made captive. We are released, liberated, which is cause for sheer joy. This is the day the Lord has made, let us rejoice and be glad in it, as we remember every Sunday, and every Sunday is a celebration of the resurrection. It was because of the resurrection of Christ that Christians switched their sabbath, the day given to God, from the Saturday to Sunday, and imbued it with a special happiness.

The passion of Christ is an expression of God's love for us and, in response to that love, we ask that we might love God in return. Furthermore, this love of God leads us to entertain one another in love. It is appropriate that in a long sequence of poems dedicated to love and marriage, it should end on such a rousing note, about the centrality of love in the teaching of Jesus.

So let us love, dear Love, like as we ought,
Love is the lesson which the Lord us taught.

Tuesday of Easter Week
I saw him standing

Ann Griffiths (translated by Rowan Williams)

Under the dark trees, there he stands,
there he stands; shall he not draw my eyes?
I thought I knew a little
how he compels, beyond all things, but now
he stands there in the shadows. It will be
Oh, such a daybreak, such bright morning,
when I shall wake to see him
as he is.

He is called Rose of Sharon, for his skin
is clear, his skin is flushed with blood,
his body lovely and exact; how he compels
beyond ten thousand rivals. There he stands,
my friend, the friend of guilt and helplessness,
to steer my hollow body
over the sea.

The earth is full of masks and fetishes,
what is there here for me? are these like him?
Keep company with him and you will know:
no kin, no likeness to those empty eyes.
He is a stranger to them all, great Jesus.
What is there here for me? I know
what I have longed for. Him to hold
me always.

Ann Griffiths (1776–1805)

Ann Griffiths lived in a small village 10 kilometres from Llanfyllin, in what is now Powys in mid North Wales. Her father was a tenant farmer and although the farm was very isolated, it was near the main coaching routes to Holyhead, London, Chester and Cardiff, so the family could be in touch with wider events. As has been remarked, they were better served by public transport then than the residents are today.

Griffiths was brought up as an Anglican but, like her brothers, she was drawn to Methodism and, in 1796, joined the Calvinistic Methodists. For most of her life, she was known by her maiden name of Ann Thomas but, after the death of both her parents, she married a young farmer, Thomas Griffiths, and they took over the family farm. She died in childbirth at the age of 29.

The area was, culturally, a very rich one. There was an emphasis on music and poetry, with its intricate Welsh forms, full of alliteration and assonance, and 73 praise poems can, with confidence, be attributed to Griffiths, of which 30 have become hymns. They were preserved by the local minister and his wife and were published after Griffiths's death. Eight letters have also survived. The poems are regarded as one of the highlights of Welsh literature, and the longest one has been described by the Welsh intellectual and dramatist Saunders Lewis as one of the great religious poems of Europe. Outwardly, Griffiths's life was short and relatively uneventful but, as another Welsh-language poet, Waldo Williams, wrote in his poem 'What is man?':

What is living? The broad hall found
Between narrow walls.

'I saw him standing', beautifully translated by Rowan Williams, who is himself a poet of distinction, begins with Griffiths seeing Christ under the dark trees in the shadow. Perhaps it was a period in her life when Christ did not seem as clear and close as he once did and she longed for the time when she would see him in the clear light of morning.

The second verse sees Christ as healthy and beautiful. The Rose of Sharon appears in the Song of Solomon as a description of 'the beloved'. Originally a love song, it came to be interpreted mystically, with Christ being the beloved and, hence, the Rose of Sharon. The verse describes how the beauty of Christ is so enthralling, so strong in its drawing power, that it can be said to compel us, as when we say that an argument in favour of something or a beautiful scene is 'compelling'. The word 'compel' appears in both the first and the second verse. This is not a compulsion achieved by coercion, but a drawing to him of our love by the sheer enchantment of the beloved. There is a paradox here: God does not compel us but the beauty of his love is compelling. As a fellow Welsh poet R. S. Thomas put it in his poem 'Perhaps':

> To yield to an unfelt pressure that irresistible
> In itself, had the character of everything
> But coercion.

The final verse expresses the sense Christians have always had of belonging to a different realm from the one too often shaped by the false values of humanity, and for which we must all take some responsibility. The world is full of the fronts we put up for other people, to hide what we are really like, and the absurd things that we think important and we cling to. Those empty eyes are so different from those of Christ, for whom the poet longs.

Wednesday of Easter Week
Easter

George Herbert

Rise heart; thy Lord is risen. Sing his praise
Without delays,
Who takes thee by the hand, that thou likewise
With him mayst rise:
That, as his death calcined thee to dust,
His life may make thee gold, and much more just.

Awake, my lute, and struggle for thy part
With all thy art.
The cross taught all wood to resound his name,
Who bore the same.
His stretched sinews taught all strings, what key
Is best to celebrate this most high day.

Consort both heart and lute, and twist a song
Pleasant and long:
Or since all music is but three parts vied
And multiplied;
O let thy blessed Spirit bear a part,
And make up our defects with his sweet art.

I got me flowers to straw thy way:
I got me boughs off many a tree:
But thou wast up by break of day,
And brought'st thy sweets along with thee.

The Sun arising in the East,
Though he give light, and th'East perfume;
If they should offer to contest
With thy arising, they presume.

Can there be any day but this,
Though many suns to shine endeavour?
We count three hundred, but we miss:
There is but one, and that one ever.

George Herbert (1593–1633)

George Herbert was part of a distinguished and cultured Welsh family, related to the Earls of Pembroke. His mother was a friend and patron of John Donne and other poets. Educated in England, he became a fellow and public orator at Cambridge, where he came to the notice of James I. For a short period, he was a member of Parliament. His thoughts turned to ordination, however, and in 1630, he became Rector of Bemerton, a small parish 75 miles south, west of London. There he wrote *A Priest to the Temple*, which sets out a wonderful ideal of rural ministry. He himself lived out this ideal, being much loved. He died of consumption only three years after taking up the appointment at Bemerton, at the age of 39.

Herbert's hymns are among the best known and loved in the English language, and his poetry expresses the quintessence of Anglican spirituality. I love his poem 'The flower' because life for all of us is one of fluctuating fortunes and changing moods. We have good times and bad. Sometimes we feel on top of the world and at other times we are full of gloom and melancholy. Herbert relates these moods to the life cycle of flowers, affirming that God is in the whole process. Sometimes, as he puts it, our shrivelled hearts are like dry, apparently dead, bulbs under the earth, but it is God who is behind this process. He can make even the tolling funeral bell one that chimes out for joy in an instant. If we could spell – that is, understand – God's language, we could see that his creative word is behind all life. It would be good if we could live as though it were spring all the time, but our sins hinder us. Then come my favourite lines:

And now in age I bud again,
After so many deaths I live and write;
I once more smell the dew and rain,
And relish versing.

We can just imagine Herbert going into his rectory garden and breathing in deeply, smelling the dew and rain. It was even more important for him than usual as, after a barren period, he could once more write poetry. In age (although he was only in his thirties!), he buds again. That poem too is good for the Easter period, but for here, I have chosen the more focused 'Easter'.

Herbert was an accomplished musician with a fine ear not just for music but also for the music of poetry. Here, both in imagery and skill, his gifts converge and enhance one another. He worked hard on the original version of this poem to bring it to perfection.[26] Scriptural themes are subtly embedded, so in the first lines we are risen with Christ (Colossians 3.1) and Christ's death reduced us to mineral dust that we might become gold through a right relationship with God, the theme of Paul's letter to the Romans. The second verse addresses the lute and in a wonderful all-embracing image, the words above the cross enable all wood to bear witness and Christ's stretched sinews teach all stringed instruments to celebrate. Music is thought of as made up of three parts, so in addition to heart and lute, the Holy Spirit is needed to make up for our defects.

This is a two-part poem, with the second part having both different imagery and a different verse form from the first part. It is the responsive song looked for in the first part, which is in the form of a religious aubade, which is a dawn song sung by a lover to wake up his beloved. The resurrection is linked to Palm Sunday. The Marys brought spices to anoint Christ's body, but he was already risen and did not need them. Then, in the fine last verse, we are encouraged to see every day in the light of the one resurrection day, which is eternal.

Thursday of Easter Week
O Sapientia
Malcolm Guite

I cannot think unless I have been thought,
Nor can I speak unless I have been spoken.
I cannot teach except as I am taught,
Or break the bread except as I am broken.
O Mind behind the mind through which I seek,
O Light within the light by which I see,
O Word beneath the words with which I speak,
O founding, unfound Wisdom, finding me,
O sounding Song whose depth is sounding me,
O Memory of time, reminding me,
My Ground of Being, always grounding me,
My Maker's Bounding Line, defining me,
Come, hidden Wisdom, come with all you bring,
Come to me now, disguised as everything.

Malcom Guite (born 1957)

Malcolm Guite was born in Nigeria, where he lived for the first ten years of his life. His first name is Ayodeji, meaning 'the second joy', suggested by the Yoruba nurse without whom he and his mother would probably have died. His parents moved to Canada, but he was educated in England, reading English Literature at Cambridge and doing a doctorate at Durham University, after which he taught for a while.

At boarding school, which he hated, Guite had strayed from the Christian faith of his childhood and adopted a combination of scientific materialism and existentialism. He gradually recovered his faith, however, through the experience of beauty in the poetry of Keats and Shelley. Guite has written that he had a religious experience when studying the Psalms as a literary text in his last year as an undergraduate, which was akin to a conversion experience. He was confirmed in the Church of England and ordained in 1991. He served in a parish and then, for many years, was a fellow and chaplain of Girton College, Cambridge.

Guite writes accessible poetry in traditional forms and, as Rowan Williams has commented, he 'knows exactly how to use the sonnet form to powerful effect' and his poems 'offer deep resources for prayer and meditation' to the reader.[27] Guite writes a weekly column for the *Church Times* and is a singer and guitarist, fronting the Cambridgeshire-based blues, rhythm and blues, and rock band Mystery Train.

Many people find it very difficult to imagine having a personal relationship with God. When he was young, the great Austin Farrer was one such person. He said that he tried hard to think of God as a person, but nothing seemed to happen. Then, as a result of reading a book by the philosopher Spinoza, he tried a different approach and, as he wrote:

> I would no longer attempt, with the psalmist, 'to set God before my face'. I would see him as the underlying cause of my thinking, especially of those thoughts in which I tried to think of him. I would dare to hope that sometimes my thought would become diaphanous, so that there should be some perception of the divine cause shining through the created effects, as a deep pool, settling into a tranquillity, permits us to see the spring in the bottom of it from which its waters rise.[28]

The poem above follows Farrer's method after Spinoza. It envisages God as the source of our thinking, speaking and everything we do. It is, in fact, a poem that was originally written for Advent, in particular for the first of the four great 'O's before Christmas, which addresses divine wisdom: *O Sapientia*. It is, however, wonderfully applicable at every time, not least when we try to think of Christ raised to a universal contemporaneity, for, as Paul made clear, Christ is the wisdom of God, who was with God from the beginning and is among us and in us now.

Christianity and Islam proclaim that God is transcendent – that is, utterly other than the universe. The religions of the Indian subcontinent like to think of God in all things. Christianity holds to both insights: God is both transcendent and immanent. It is not pantheistic – a view which holds that God and the world are one. It is, however, pan*en*theistic, believing that the transcendent God is also in and through all things. As mentioned in an earlier discussion, this is the view that comes across in some of Wordsworth's poems.

This lovely, profound sonnet by Guite can be said slowly, savoured and meditated on for a long time.

Friday of Easter Week
Shadows

D. H. Lawrence

And if to-night my soul may find her peace
in sleep, and sink in good oblivion,
and in the morning wake like a new-opened flower
then I have been dipped again in God, and new created.

And if, as weeks go round, in the dark of the moon
my spirit darkens and goes out, and soft strange gloom
pervades my movements and my thoughts and words
then shall I know that I am walking still
with God, we are close together now the moon's in shadow.

And if, as autumn deepens and darkens
I feel the pain of falling leaves, and stems that break in
        storms
and trouble and dissolution and distress
and then the softness of deep shadows folding, folding
around my soul and spirit, around my lips
so sweet, like a swoon, or more like the drowse of a low, sad
        song
singing darker than the nightingale, on, on to the solstice
and the silence of short days, the silence of the year, the
        shadow,
then I shall know that my life is moving still
with the dark earth, and drenched
with the deep oblivion of earth's lapse and renewal.

And if, in the changing phases of man's life
I fall in sickness and in misery
my wrists seem broken and my heart seems dead
and strength is gone, and my life
is only the leavings of a life:

and still, among it all, snatches of lovely oblivion, and
    snatches of renewal
odd, wintry flowers upon the withered stem, yet new,
    strange flowers
such as my life has not brought forth before, new blossoms
    of me,
then I must know that still
I am in the hands of the unknown God,
he is breaking me down to his own oblivion
to send me forth on a new morning, a new man.

D. H. Lawrence (1885–1930)

D. H. Lawrence became notorious with the publication in 1920 of *The Rainbow* and *Women in Love*, which openly explore the physical relationship of human beings in a way that led to the novels being banned at the time. His novel *Lady Chatterley's Lover* was the subject of a famous trial in 1960, when the publishers were charged under the Obscene Publications Act and found not guilty. This notoriety has detracted from two important aspects of Lawrence's work. First, he was an outstanding poet as well as a novelist, writing more than 800 poems. Second, he had an interesting, ambivalent relationship with the Christian faith. Like Dr Johnson, he exposed romantic talk about poverty,[29] and his understanding of humility, for example, is much more to the point than most sermonic expositions.[30] He also had an important understanding of death, writing in one poem that if we cannot sing the song of death, we cannot sing the song of life.[31]

The poem above has been one of my favourites for many decades and it would follow on well from a reading of George Herbert's 'The flower' (see my brief discussion in the section on George Herbert, pages 160–1). Both of them compare human life to plants, but Lawrence widens the image out to include not just the cycle of the seasons but also the whole life cycle of human beings, including those periods of depression when all we seem to have are 'the leavings of a life'. His theme is that all the periods of darkness, whether sleep at night or times when we seem bereft of everything worthwhile, are times of renewal, even when we are reduced to what he calls oblivion. Indeed, he goes beyond Herbert's poem in suggesting not only that we can bud again but also that these times bring forth:

> odd, wintry flowers upon the withered stem, yet new,
> strange flowers
> such as my life has not brought forth before, new blossoms
> of me.

Lawrence suggests that in all these parts of the human cycle of life we are in the hands of God.

> I am in the hands of the unknown God,
> he is breaking me down to his own oblivion
> to send me forth on a new morning, a new man.

From a Christian point of view, though God is, as Lawrence rightly says, unknown in himself, he has also made himself known to us in human form, in a human face and heart. The unknown is made humanly known in Jesus risen, ascended and glorified, who raises us to new life every morning and will raise us again on the last day. Every day he sends us forth newly created in him, a new person, ready for 'new blossoms of me'.

Saturday of Easter Week
Sailing to Byzantium

William Butler Yeats

I

That is no country for old men. The young
In one another's arms, birds in the trees,
– Those dying generations – at their song,
The salmon-falls, the mackerel-crowded seas,
Fish, flesh, or fowl, commend all summer long
Whatever is begotten, born, and dies.
Caught in that sensual music all neglect
Monuments of unageing intellect.

II

An aged man is but a paltry thing,
A tattered coat upon a stick, unless
Soul clap its hands and sing, and louder sing
For every tatter in its mortal dress,
Nor is there singing school but studying
Monuments of its own magnificence;
And therefore I have sailed the seas and come
To the holy city of Byzantium.

III

O sages standing in God's holy fire
As in the gold mosaic of a wall,
Come from the holy fire, perne in a gyre,
And be the singing-masters of my soul.

Consume my heart away; sick with desire
And fastened to a dying animal
It knows not what it is; and gather me
Into the artifice of eternity.

IV
Once out of nature I shall never take
My bodily form from any natural thing,
But such a form as Grecian goldsmiths make
Of hammered gold and gold enamelling
To keep a drowsy Emperor awake;
Or set upon a golden bough to sing
To lords and ladies of Byzantium
Of what is past, or passing, or to come.

William Butler Yeats (1865–1939)

Yeats spent his early years in Sligo, on the west coast of Ireland, where he imbibed deeply of the local myths and legends. He became, and remained all his life, a strong believer in magic and all forms of occultism. Most people regard such notions as intellectually vacuous, but they freed Yeats's imagination and enabled him to create mesmerizing poetry that lures the reader into an almost drug-induced state, as in this poem. In fact, so powerful is its effect that some aspiring poets, such as the young R. S. Thomas, knew that they had fiercely to put Yeats's poetry aside in order to find their own voice.

Yeats hated getting old. At 69, he had surgery to restore his sexual potency. He wrote:

You think it horrible that lust and rage
Should dance attention upon my old age;
They were not such a plague when I was young;
What else have I to spur me into song?

'Sailing to Byzantium' is such a song that he was spurred into. His words I quoted earlier in relation to Donne are apt here too: 'We make out of the quarrel with others, rhetoric, and out of the quarrel with ourselves, poetry'. This poem is very much a quarrel with himself, a horrifying realization that he was getting old – indeed, that in due course, he was going to die, as we all do – and, at the same time, an awareness that he still had a reservoir of creativity within him. It is a poem that entered deeply into the psyche of the twentieth century. I have spotted four phrases in it that became the title of a book or film or both and there may be more. It is a poem of glorious phrases, the combination of image and sound taking the reader into another dimension. Poetry is itself and cannot be translated into anything else, we just let it work its effect on us, but here is a very simple analysis of the poem in the plainest prose.

The poem begins by recognizing that the world of young people falling in love and the many sensual delights of youth is no place for old men. That is because, in such a world, what the old have to offer is neglected. What they have to offer is creative intelligence, which can create works of art that last. So he will leave that world of sensual pleasures, which part of him so desires.

The second verse paints a vivid picture of an old man as no more than a scarecrow, but then comes the brilliant caveat. With every sign of decrepitude, we can learn to sing. In order to do this, we have to study the great works of art of the past, so the poet sails to Byzantium (Istanbul today).

In Byzantium there stands the great Hagia Sophia, built by Justinian in the sixth century, with its fragments of once glorious mosaics of saints and kings. He asks these to be singing-masters of his soul, so that, though he is dying, he might create works of eternal worth.

In the final verse, Yeats imagines those glorious works, and how he will produce them and enchant others with them.

This is not just a poem about a talented artist, but one about and for each one of us. For each one of us has a spark of creativity. There is a poem by Rudyard Kipling, 'When earth's last picture is painted', in which he thinks of everyone as an artist:

> And no one shall work for money, and no one shall work
>   for fame,
> But each for the joy of the working, and each, in his sepa-
>   rate star,
> Shall draw the Thing as he sees It for the God of Things as
>   They are!

That creativity does not have to be expressed only in art or music or writing. Millions of people express it in the care they put into their gardening or cooking. That spark of creativity is part of what we mean by being made in the image of God.

Furthermore, none of us, as we get older, is free of the sense of loss as we slow down and can no longer do what we once did. Somehow, we have to learn to sing for every tatter in our mortal dress. Very difficult it is, if we are feeling old and achy or much worse. From a Christian point of view, we do not look to 'sages standing in God's holy fire' only as works of art but also as holy ones, in whom we see the artifice of eternity. We learn to sing as they sing – that is, in tune with the music of God. It is in this way, as Paul writes, that we become God's work of art, his *poiema* (Ephesians 2.10).

Second Sunday of Easter
This world is not conclusion

Emily Dickinson

This World is not Conclusion.
A Species stands beyond –
Invisible, as Music –
But positive, as Sound –
It beckons, and it baffles –
Philosophy, don't know –
And through a Riddle, at the last -
Sagacity, must go –
To guess it, puzzles scholars –
To gain it, Men have borne
Contempt of Generations
And Crucifixion, shown –
Faith slips – and laughs, and rallies –
Blushes, if any see –
Plucks at a twig of Evidence –
And asks a Vane, the way –
Much Gesture, from the Pulpit –
Strong Hallelujahs roll –
Narcotics cannot still the Tooth
That nibbles at the soul –

Emily Dickinson (1830–1886)

Emily Dickinson lived a quiet, reclusive life in Amherst, Massachusetts. She had an ambivalent relationship with her local church and this was, I believe, because the intensity of her own inner experience made what went on in it seem to her so much idle chatter. She created her own unique poetic style and is now generally thought to be, with Walt Whitman, one of, America's most important nineteenth-century poets. Her punctuation and syntax generally are unique, with sometimes a single word expected to stand for a whole phrase. Particular attention needs to be paid to her dashes. They indicate a pause or brief silence in which what has gone before resonates in the mind.

In the poem above, the first four lines could not be more positive. There is a world beyond this one, a world of angels that, like music, we cannot see but is just as real. It is clear from so many of her poems that this world was indeed very real for her. This world, as it says in the fifth line, draws us to it; it beckons us. It also baffles us, however, because we can never quite grasp or understand it.

The next four lines show that bafflement. Philosophy leaves us agnostic: scholars can spend a lifetime studying and still not come up with a firm answer. However wise or sagacious people think they are, they come up against a riddle. But, as the subsequent four lines indicate, people are still willing to bear contempt and rejection for their faith, so although we may slip, we can still laugh and rally.

The following four lines show Dickinson at her most puckish and ironic. Although most of her poems come over as very serious, with a strong emphasis on death, she has this wry self-knowledge and humour as well. She is shy about her faith and does not want others to catch the intensity of it, but she knows how prone we all are to wishful thinking, plucking at any twig of evidence to support our views. Then, in a wonderful brief image, she imagines what is going on in church, the preacher gesturing a lot to make up for his real lack of conviction, this being echoed by hallelujahs in the congregation.

The final two lines are a teaser. What is the tooth that nibbles at the soul? Is it the doubt that can gnaw at us, with religion being a narcotic? Is it, instead, the other world we catch in glimpses, as Dickinson asserts in the first few lines, that will always haunt us – the conviction that this world is not all; that there is another realm, another dimension, another form of being, one presently just beyond our grasp?

Monday
Signs

Piers Plowright

Some sentences leap out
of the Big Black Book
like friends:
'Supposing him to be the gardener'
'Did not our hearts burn within us?'
'Come and have breakfast' –
Divine ends

dressed in the everyday:
gardener, lover, cook,
standing in for God,
the truth not far away
but near as breath:
fruit, fire, charcoaled fish
holding the Word.

These signs seem right
to me:
no cloud, no lightning flash, no mystery,
no 'Unknown God' to puzzle out.
But something real, solid,
near-at-hand –
and free.

Piers Plowright (1937–2021)

After a short period working for the British Council in the Sudan, Piers Plowright spent the whole of his working life as a BBC producer. Rejecting all overtures to move into management and promotion, he stuck to what he knew and loved. Initially in drama (for he was a talented actor), he moved to documentaries. As Melvyn Bragg put it: 'His fascination for people and the situations they find themselves in sparked his flair for capturing voices and sounds.'[32] In addition to producing a round of familiar programmes, he developed and perfected his unique sound pictures. These were situated in such unlikely places as a Jewish delicatessen in Philadelphia. Using background noises and the occasional interview, he succeeded in creating his own mini-art form. This was recognized by his peers, for he won the Prix Italia for radio drama and documentaries three times, and six Sony awards, including one for his special contribution to radio. Always avoiding overtly moral or didactic purposes, he liked to put together ordinary sounds in a way that conveyed something unique to the listener, something that, if we opened our ears and listened to more, we ourselves might hear in the ordinary round of experience.

He was married to Dr Poh Sim, one of the world's leading specialists in Noh drama, which, he said, helped him to understand better the role of silence in his work. The quality of silence in a convent he once visited was also one of the reasons he became a Roman Catholic. The writer Rupert Shortt, noting Plowright's great *joie de vivre*, wrote that behind it 'stood a faith that supplied an extra dimension to all else in his life. It was at once simple, subtle and life-enhancing.'[33] This faith helped him through the years in which cancer took a growing hold of his life.

For Piers Plowright, to live was to create. Every day for most of his life, he wrote a diary, complete with his sketches; right to the end, he was producing what he disparagingly called his 'doodles', together with poems, mostly short and sometimes fragmentary. His personality was always positive, always cheerful, radiating the strong lines and bright colours that were a feature of his paintings, even when he was very ill.

'Signs' was written and sent to *The Tablet* just before his death in July 2021. The first verse picks out some of the key statements from appearances of the risen Christ that resonate in the mind: one to Mary Magdalene in the garden; one on the road to Emmaus; and a third on the Lake of Galilee. Then, just as his radio work showed something special in the most ordinary settings, he lets these appearances lead us to see Christ in what is familiar: as 'gardener, lover, cook'. Whereas those of a mystical or philosophical frame of mind might at that point have gone off into the abstract, the poem almost pushes our faces into the tangible and material. It is a profoundly sacramental view of the world in which the outward and material disclose the spiritual, and in which the eternal God comes to us in the everyday. As George Herbert put it in his poem 'Prayer. (I)', this is 'heaven in ordinary'. This is a God who is 'near-at-hand' and freely given to us in what is around us, in detail that we take for granted.

Tuesday
Little Gidding

T. S. Eliot

With the drawing of this Love and the voice of this Calling

We shall not cease from exploration
And the end of all our exploring
Will be to arrive where we started
And know the place for the first time.
Through the unknown, unremembered gate
When the last of earth left to discover
Is that which was the beginning;
At the source of the longest river
The voice of the hidden waterfall
And the children in the apple-tree
Not known, because not looked for
But heard, half-heard, in the stillness
Between two waves of the sea.
Quick now, here, now, always –
A condition of complete simplicity
(Costing not less than everything)
And all shall be well and
All manner of thing shall be well
When the tongues of flames are in-folded
Into the crowned knot of fire
And the fire and the rose are one.

T. S. Eliot (1888–1965)

T. S. Eliot was brought up in St Louis, at the confluence of the Mississippi and Missouri rivers, but his family roots were in Boston, where his family had emigrated to from Britain in the seventeenth century. Images from these happy years appear later in his poetry. After Harvard, he went to Oxford in 1914 to finish his doctorate in philosophy. His modernist masterpiece 'The love song of J. Alfred Prufrock' was published in 1915. Later, he became a British citizen.

Eliot's poetry changed people's whole understanding of what counts as poetry and his criticism resulted in a new appreciation of formerly neglected poets, especially those of the seventeenth century. His poem *The Waste Land* (1922) expressed not only the pain of his own unhappy marriage but also the sense of disillusion and lostness of the times. He quickly shed the Unitarianism in which he had been brought up and, in 1927, he was baptized as an Anglican, a turning point reflected in *Ash-Wednesday*. In later life, he remained hugely influential as a publisher at Faber and Faber and something of a sage on issues of literature, faith and society. He wrote a number of verse dramas but, except for *Murder in the Cathedral*, they did not receive the acclaim of his poetry. He was awarded the Nobel Prize in Literature in 1948.

The *Four Quartets*, published between 1936 and 1942, reflected Eliot's mature Christian faith. The excerpt above is the last section of the fifth movement of the final quartet. As the title implies, these poems are like music, in that they state a theme, which then recurs with many variations. In these climactic verses, earlier themes find a wonderful resolution. The mystery of time is one major theme. We reflect on the past and wonder about the future but, for the poem, the point of time is to usher us into the present moment, which intersects with the timeless. We move with time and are different now from what we were in the past and what we will be in the future. In this now we can be still, at the still point of the turning world. This is both our starting point and our end point. Here, the images of some tantalizing delight just out of reach, perhaps associated with childhood, have their place. We experience the drawing of a love and the voice of a calling (words from the fourteenth-century mystical book *The Cloud of Unknowing*), but we have to catch this moment and respond to it with a total handing over of our lives.

Quick now, here, now, always –
A condition of complete simplicity
(Costing not less than everything)

Eliot owned a copy of *The Spiritual Letters of Dom John Chapman O.S.B*, first published in 1935. Chapman was much influenced by *Self-Abandonment to Divine Providence* by Jean-Pierre de Caussade,[34] first published in English in 1933, whose whole emphasis is on accepting the present moment as the will of God – the sacrament of the present moment, which, simply, is abandoning oneself to the will of God moment by moment.

Chapman has the phrase 'oraison de simple remise' in a letter of 1920,[35] which could be understood as a prayer of simple handing over, and this sheds light on Eliot's words, 'A condition of complete simplicity/(costing not less than everything).' At that point of complete handing over, we know, with Julian of Norwich (another fourteenth-century mystic), that 'all shall be well'. In the final image, based on some verses at the end of Dante's *Paradiso,* the flame of divine love (which is also the lacerating fire of painful self-knowledge) is at one with the rose of redeemed humanity.[36] The rose is an image that recurs throughout the poem with different associations. Here it is the white rose of Dante, which is an image of redeemed humanity. Dante had written:

Within the depths I saw ingathered, bound by love in one
volume, the scattered leaves of the universe; substance and

accidents and their relations, as though together fused, after such fashion that what I tell of is one simple flame.[37]

This flame comes together in a sailor's knot, the three strands of which form a Trinity. In that knot, love, human and divine, are united. This echoes some other lines in *The Cloud of Unknowing*: 'Knit the ghostly knot of burning love betwixt thee and thy God, in ghostly onehead and according of will.'[38]

This unity of love between God and humanity is where all our searching and striving is leading. Earlier in the *Four Quartets*, in 'East Coker', Eliot had written that old men ought to be explorers, and that, rooted in a stillness which is also a movement, we must venture into 'a further union, a deeper communion'.

Notes

1 Richard Harries, *The One Genius: Readings through the year with Austin Farrer* (London: SPCK, 1987), p. 50.

2 Ulrich Simon, *Pity and Terror: Christianity and tragedy* (London: Macmillan, 1989), p. 64.

3 T. S. Eliot, *Selected Prose* (Faber, 1975), p. 243.

4 For more on Auden, see Richard Harries, *Haunted by Christ: Modern writers and the struggle for faith* (London: SPCK, 2018), pp. 97 ff.

5 From Elizabeth Jennings, *New Collected Poems* (London: Carcanet Press, 2002), p. xix, which Michael Schmidt, a poet and the founder of Carcanet Press, edited.

6 Harries, *Haunted by Christ*, pp. 155 ff.

7 R. S. Thomas, *Song at the Year's Turning* (London: Rupert Hart-Davis, 1955), p. 14.

8 Harries, *Haunted by Christ*, p. 123 ff.

9 Hephzibah Anderson, 'Christmas carol', *The Observer*, 4 December 2005.

10 Harries, *Haunted by Christ*, Chapter 4.

11 Harries, *Haunted by Christ*, Chapter 4.

12 C. S. Lewis writes wonderfully about this in his spiritual autobiography *Surprised by Joy* and in his wartime essay 'The weight of glory'.

13 Letter to Sir George Beaumont, 28 May 1825.

14 See Richard Harries, *Art and the Beauty of God: A Christian understanding* (London: Mowbray, 1993), p. 6.

15 Michael Bennett and Vanessa D. Dickerson, *Recovering the Black Female Body: Self-representations by African American women* (New Brunswick, NJ: Rutgers University Press, 2001), p. 127.

16 Langston Hughes, 'The Negro artist and the racial mountain', *The Nation*, 23 June 1926, pp. 692–3.

17 Richard Harries, *The Beauty and the Horror: Searching for God in a suffering world* (London: SPCK, 2016), pp. 151 ff.

18 Harries, *Haunted by Christ*, pp. 32 ff.

19 Edwin Muir, *An Autobiography* (London: Hogarth, 1987), pp. 277–8.

20 Muir, *An Autobiography,* p. 280.

21 Harries, *Haunted by Christ*, pp. 140 ff.

22 Charles Marsh, *Strange Glory: A life of Dietrich Bonhoeffer* (New York: Alfred K. Knopf, 2014), p. 284.

23 See Richard Harries, *The Passion in Art* (Aldershot: Ashgate, 2004), pp. 24ff.

24 William Langland, *The Book Concerning Piers Plowman*, Donald and Rachel Attwater (trans.), Rachel Attwater (ed.) (London: J. M. Dent, Everyman Library, 1957), pp. 17–18.

25 See Harries, *The Passion in Art*, pp. 31 ff. and 87 ff.

26 John Drury, *Music at Midnight: The life and poetry of George Herbert* (London: Allen Lane, 2014), pp. 142–4.

27 On the cover of Malcolm Guite's book *Sounding the Seasons* (Norwich: Canterbury Press, 2012).

28 Austin Farrer, *The Glass of Vision* (London: Dacre Press, 1948), pp. 7–8.

29 D. H. Lawrence, *The Rainbow* (London: Heinemann, 1955), p. 282.

30 D. H. Lawrence, 'Tender reverence', *Complete Poems*, Vol. II, Vivian de sola Pinto and Warren Roberts (eds) (London: Heineman, 1964), p. 622.

31 'Song of death', *Complete Poems*, Vol. II, p. 723.

32 Melvyn Bragg, 'Piers Plowright obituary', *The Guardian*, 12 August 2021.

33 Rupert Shortt, 'Word from the Cloisters: The joy of the muddle', *The Tablet*, 7 August 2021, p. 16.

34 *The Spiritual Letters of Dom John Chapman, O. S. B.* (New York: Sheed & Ward, 1946); Jean-Pierre de Caussade, *Self-Abandonment to Divine Providence*, Algar Thorold (trans.) (London: Collins, 1971).

35 *Spiritual Letters*, p. 60.

36 Harries, *Haunted by Christ*, pp. 61ff.

37 Dante Alighieri, *The Divine Comedy: Paradiso*, Canto XXXIII: 85–93.

38 Justin McCann (ed.), *The Cloud of Unknowing and Other Treatises* (London: Burns, Oates & Washbourne, 1924), ch. 2.

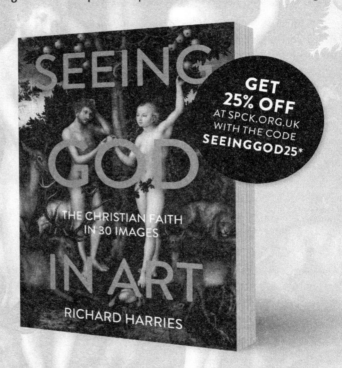